The Road Well Travelled

Also by the same author and available from Canterbury Press

Seasons of the Son: A journey through the Christian year
978–185311–884–5

www.canterburypress.co.uk

The Road Well Travelled

Exploring traditional Christian spirituality

David Winter

CANTERBURY
PRESS
Norwich

© David Winter 2009

First published in 2009 by the Canterbury Press Norwich
Editorial office
13–17 Long Lane,
London, EC1A 9PN, UK

Canterbury Press is an imprint of Hymns Ancient and
Modern Ltd (a registered charity)
St Mary's Works, St Mary's Plain,
Norwich, NR3 3BH, UK

www.scm-canterburypress.co.uk

Scripture quotations are from the New Revised Standard
Version of the Bible, copyright 1989 by the Division of
Christian Education of the National Council of the Churches
of Christ in the USA. Used by permission. All rights reserved.

British Library Cataloguing in Publication data

A catalogue record for this book is available
from the British Library

978-1-85311-964-4

Typeset by Regent Typesetting, London
Printed and bound in Great Britain by
CPI Bookmarque, Croydon CR0 4TD

CONTENTS

INTRODUCTION

There's a rather tired old cliché about 'throwing the baby away with the bath-water' – ditching something valuable in the process of disposing of something unwanted. Like all clichés, it enshrines a truth, and that truth is as relevant in the area of Christian spirituality as it is in politics, commerce or the law. Valuable insights, treasured ways of doing things, even proven paths to God, have been abandoned not because they were unworthy or unhelpful, but because of their associations. So, to give an example, someone who is uneasy about Catholic veneration of the Blessed Virgin Mary needlessly excludes her from every aspect of their devotions, denying themselves a wonderful model of Christian obedience, love and discipleship. The veneration of Mary on the one hand, and her role as a model of discipleship on the other, are two different issues, two different things entirely, but they have come to be seen as part of a 'package'.

I suppose this book is about rescuing that wretched baby, because it is arrogance and folly to abandon old and treasured ways simply because those who practise them today are 'not one of us'. In truth, all who belong to Christ are 'one of us', and we can all learn from each other on that long and sometimes painful path of the pilgrim. After all, the word 'catholic' simply means 'general' or 'universal', and was adopted by the early Church as its chosen title to distinguish it from various sects and heresies which had sprung up around it. In that sense, all orthodox Christians are 'Catholics' – they believe what the apostles believed, they see themselves as part of the Church which Jesus brought into being on that foundation. It was not until the great rift between the Eastern ('Orthodox') Church and the Western 'Catholic' Church that the title was applied to any specific association of churches – and not until the Reformation that the largest of those 'associations' became known distinctively as the 'Roman Catholic Church'.

So, in its original meaning, we are all 'catholic', and the rich tradition of the Catholic faith founded by the apostles and practised by holy men and women down the centuries is ours. From our own positions we may feel remote from that tradition, but in truth it belongs to all of us. Perhaps the time has come for us to look beyond our own spiritual boxes and explore the treasures on the other side of the wall.

And what treasures they are! Few would deny that the Catholic tradition in Christianity has bred many wonderful saints, men and women who have lived sacrificially, borne faithful witness to the gospel, denied themselves and 'taken up the cross' to follow Jesus. We may find the language of medieval devotion difficult, even disturbing. It is not part of the devotional life of Evangelicals to talk of being 'hidden in the wounds of Jesus', though they are happy to speak of being 'washed in the blood of the Lamb'. Many of them feel awkward when others speak of eating the flesh of Christ or drinking his blood, even though Jesus himself said that these were essential to receiving his life (see John 6.54). There may be more than one way of interpreting these words and metaphors, but there is tremendous power in the fundamental message that they convey about the relationship of the Christian believer to the crucified and risen Lord Jesus.

Over the years I have met many people in the evangelical tradition, like myself, who have explored these treasures. They have found in various aspects of Catholic spirituality enormous help and inspiration. This does not mean that they have lost their own distinctive perspective on the gospel, far from it; neither has it required them to accept Roman Catholic beliefs about such things as the Assumption, transubstantiation or papal infallibility. But they have, if you like, 'cherry-picked' the rich fruit of a historic and honoured spirituality. They are now drinking from the same well as Bernard of Clairvaux, Hildegard of Bingen, Mother Julian, Francis and Clare. They have tapped a vein of spirituality, a way of being Christian, that has run like a thread through the entire history of the Christian Church.

This book is about that thread, that 'well-travelled road' that has brought discipline, blessing, healing and renewal to so many of those who have walked it before us. It would be tragic if some modern Christians were to close their minds to the possibility that what has nourished generations of saints was somehow out of bounds to Christians who wear a different 'label' but bear the same Name.

David Winter
Advent 2008

I

WAYS OF READING THE BIBLE

Lectio divina

It seems sensible to begin on common ground, the Bible. All Christians recognize the unique nature of the Scriptures and to varying degrees accept their authority as the touchstone of Christian belief and practice. Every Christian service includes at least one, usually several, readings from the Bible. Sermons, addresses and homilies pick up its themes and its message. Every Christian home has as a cherished possession a copy, or many copies, of the Bible – and in some of them they are read regularly.

In the second letter to Timothy there is a short list of the ways in which the Scriptures are 'useful'. (The Scriptures referred to are of course the Hebrew Scriptures, because the New Testament didn't yet exist.) They are, the writer claims, 'useful for teaching, reproof, correction and training in righteousness, so that everyone who belongs to God may be proficient, equipped for every good work' (2 Timothy 3.16–17).

So the Bible is 'useful'; it trains, corrects, equips. And that is probably how most of us see it: a manual of instruction, guidance, correction and encouragement. However, all through the history of the Church a way of reading the

Bible has been practised which seems to transcend all of those uses – or, perhaps, weaves them into a spiritual experience which is much greater than the sum total of the parts. It is true that we read the Bible for 'information' about the faith ('teaching'). We read it for ethical and moral warning and guidance ('reproof, correction, training in righteousness'). We read it to equip us for God's service ('every good work').

Yet the New Testament itself recognizes another way of reading the Bible. Ancient tradition calls it *lectio divina* – literally, 'divine' or spiritual reading. It offers a kind of catalyst which makes possible a different, though not contradictory, approach to Scripture. There's an example of it in St Paul's letter to the Christians at Colosse. They are told to 'let the word of Christ dwell in you richly' (3.16). The word 'richly' here is very strong. It implies a fullness, an overflowing. His hearers are to be saturated with the word of Christ (presumably the teaching of Jesus and the stories of his life, death and resurrection). The 'word' is to soak into the readers' or listeners' hearts and minds – as one person put it to me, like a rich sherry soaking down into the dull sponge at the bottom of a trifle and transforming it. The letter of Peter and the letter to the Hebrews both speak similarly of the word of God as 'living and active', an organism rather than a book.

However we describe this 'other way' of opening ourselves to the Bible, it is much more than opening its pages to find information, answers to questions, or even ethical guidance. This way is more like an engagement with a living being, opening ourselves to a dynamic encounter with the One who is the source of all being.

This way of reading the Bible is not concerned with questions of textual or literary analysis. It doesn't even ask the usual questions (how? when? by whom?). The reader simply opens himself or herself to the Scripture in what Lesslie Newbigin called its 'canonical form' and listens to its inner voice. That is not to dismiss biblical scholarship, or to say that we should never grapple with the text or use the tools of scholarly research to uncover its meaning or appreciate the particular idiom or literary form in which it is expressed. But it is to say that if that is the *only* way we ever read the Scripture then we are missing much of its divine purpose. It wasn't written for the library or the lecture theatre, but to enable ordinary believers to meet with God, to hear his voice, to enter into a rich, living relationship with him, a kind of conversation of the soul.

That may all sound rather precious. In fact it is no more than the 'other side' of prayer. In prayer, we think of ourselves as talking to God. In *lectio divina* we think of God talking to us. One is, on the whole, a speaking exercise; the other is a listening one. When we turn to this kind of Bible reading, our primary responsibility is to listen – *really* listen. We open ourselves to the divine voice, keeping still and surrendered to the task. Like Elijah on Mount Horeb, our ears need to be attuned. The earthquake and the storm (the events and pressures of the day, the clamour of life) dominate. It is only when they are stilled that we can hear what the Bible calls 'the sound of sheer silence' (1 Kings 19.12). That seems like a total contradiction: sound from silence. Yet in that profound silence the prophet heard the message of God, 'loud and clear', as we say.

So to use the Scriptures in this particular way, we shall need to bring certain qualities to it. We shall need attention, the focus of mind and spirit on the text before us. We shall need reflection, as we allow its message to infiltrate into our thinking until it saturates our minds and wills. We shall need to apply what we then hear to our own lives and circumstances, and finally we shall need to obey whatever it says to us.

Space and silence are not easily acquired commodities in modern life, and people have told me that the absence of them is an important factor in inhibiting their own interior spiritual life. However, others have found that 'those who seek, find': that space is more about mental discipline than square metres, and that silence is more than simply the absence of noise. To engage in *lectio* we shall need to create that space and silence, even if we live in cramped conditions and noise is more or less incessant (as it often is today). Somewhere, somehow, we shall find a place and time to hide away with the Word of God and listen to his voice.

This is dynamic Bible reading, allowing the Word of God to permeate our being. It doesn't require a fundamentalist view of Scripture, simply a belief that through this text in some way (which we may not be able to categorize) God speaks to his people 'heart to heart'. After all, he has done it for thousands of years, and as they have listened he has spoken. There will be time enough and many occasions in which to encounter Scripture in different ways, using it to wrestle with the profound truths of faith, or to teach and instruct us in Christian discipleship. Here, with a narrower, more intense focus, we seek from the text just one thing, but that the greatest thing a human being can ask for: a living relationship with a living God.

An exercise in *lectio*

And after Jesus had dismissed the crowds, he went up the mountain by himself to pray. When evening came, he was there alone, but by this time the boat, battered by the waves, was far from the land, for the wind was against them.

And early in the morning he came walking toward them on the sea. But when the disciples saw him walking on the sea, they were terrified, saying, 'It is a ghost!' And they cried out in fear. But immediately Jesus spoke to them and said, 'Take heart, it is I; do not be afraid.'

Peter answered him, 'Lord, if it is you, command me to come to you on the water.' He said, 'Come.' So Peter got out of the boat, started walking on the water, and came toward Jesus. But when he noticed the strong wind, he became frightened, and beginning to sink, he cried out, 'Lord, save me!' Jesus immediately reached out his hand and caught him, saying to him, 'You of little faith, why did you doubt?'

When they got into the boat, the wind ceased. And those in the boat worshipped him, saying, 'Truly you are the Son of God.'

Matthew 14.22–33

1 Simply read the passage. Try not to be distracted by all the modern questions: Did he really walk on water? How did he do it? How could Peter do it, too, even if only briefly? Instead, just absorb the text; listen to the story.
2 Re-read it, as many times as you can. Listen to the inner voice of the text.
3 Imagine the scene: the familiar lake suddenly turned enemy, the quiet waters threatening to overturn the boat, the wind against them so that they could make no headway. Does it sound familiar? Is this what life often feels like?
4 Visualize the impact of the appearance of Jesus – 'it is I', *ego eimi*: 'I am'.
5 Absorb the astounding truth that Jesus came to them walking on their fears, on the very waters that threatened to overwhelm them.
6 Quietly thank God for whatever he has said to you. Note it, accept it, and respond to it.

Each reader will have a uniquely personal encounter both with the text and with God himself. There are many other things in the story (Peter's reaction, for instance) but this is not a Bible study, just an exercise in listening to the text.

2

PRAYING WITH THE
WHOLE CHURCH

The communion of saints

At any given moment, there are obviously more Christians in heaven than there are on earth – many, many more. What are we to make of this vast unseen army of the 'saints', those who in past ages, and in our time, too, have put their faith in Jesus? Do we simply forget them, ignore them, tell ourselves that 'they're all right anyway' and simply get on with our earthly lives? Or does their existence mean something to us; affect the way we live, pray and witness? What, in other words, is the significance of the 'communion of saints' to which the Creed bears testimony?

Probably the first thing to say is that 'communion' simply means 'fellowship' (*koinonia*, in Greek). To believe in 'the communion of saints' is to assert that we are still in 'fellowship' with those who have died. We are here and they are 'there', but we are all 'in Christ', we are all bound together in the love of God.

But how do we express this fellowship? The hymn 'The Church's one foundation' speaks of 'mystic, sweet communion with those whose rest is won' – but that may well seem rather vague and even sentimental to a twenty-first-century Christian. In what way are we 'one' with them? How can we have 'fellowship' with people most of whom we don't know, have never met and who may have lived many centuries ago? Is the whole idea so fanciful that there's no point in pursuing it?

We can see fewer problems where those we have loved are concerned. Down the centuries most Christians have in one way or another related to those they have known who have died. This may be no more than sometimes thankfully remembering them before God, or trying in our lives to follow the example of faith which they set us. If they are people we have loved deeply, it may go much further than that. We may be acutely aware of the reality of their continuing life, even feel that they are near us in our everyday routines. Each of these responses is, in some way, a reflection of the reality of the 'communion of saints'.

That, of course, raises the question of prayer for or about those who have died. This has been an issue from the earliest days of the Church, or at any rate from the time when Christians realized that the return of Jesus Christ to earth might be long delayed. Even Monica, the saintly mother of St Augustine, was rebuked by her bishop for what he saw as her superstitious practice of putting cakes and drink in the tombs of dead Christians. There is no clear example of prayer for those who have died in the New Testament, though the reference to Onesiphorus (2 Timothy 1.18) certainly implies it.

The Churches of the Reformation have, on the whole, been reluctant to encourage, or even sanction, prayers 'for' the dead. That is to say, they reject the idea that our prayers can in some way improve the lot of those who have died in Christ. The principle behind this is simple: if they are 'in Christ' and (in St Paul's words) 'with Christ' (Philippians 1.23), it seems almost blasphemous to think that our prayers can 'improve' the joy and perfection of heaven for them.

This antipathy to prayers for those who have died arose out of the situation in the medieval Church, where there was a whole industry engaged in encouraging and providing prayers and masses for the departed, generally at a price. The dark shadow hanging behind this was, of course, the doctrine of purgatory – the time and place where those not yet ready for the perfection of heaven could be purged from their unforgiven sins. It was assumed that earthly prayers and masses could help to shorten this painful experience. Such practices have been generally abandoned in the Roman Catholic Church in recent times, though the principle has been retained that the living may 'intercede' for the dead.

But it is not only the Roman Catholics who have been reviewing their beliefs and practices where those who have died are concerned. Many evangelical Christians have realized that not all prayer is intercessory prayer – indeed, perhaps the richest form of prayer is simply relational, the building of a sense of fellowship between the believer and God, the sharing of hopes, fears, longings and most of all love. Into that prayer of relationship, it must surely be possible to include our love for those we have known on earth but see with earthly eyes no longer.

We may not feel any need to pray *for* them, believing that to be with Christ – again, as St Paul says – is 'far better'; but we can pray *about* them, holding them in God's love, enjoying in prayer our assurance that they are secure in his presence. In that way, we can enjoy our continuing fellowship with them, because both we and they are 'in Christ'. We can constantly thank God for our memories of them and for the impact of their lives on ours. We can express our 'joyful hope' in the coming day of resurrection, when in some way beyond our present understanding we and they will be reunited in the kingdom of heaven.

The communion of saints goes beyond that, of course, inviting us to see ourselves as part of the vast fellowship of all God's people, 'living and departed in the Lord Jesus', as the Funeral Service says, from the days of the apostles until the end of time. It is *more* than realizing afresh our fellowship with those we have known who have died 'in Christ' – but it isn't *less*. Reflecting on the lesser may help us to enter into the wonder of the greater, the awesome privilege of being part of that 'multitude that no one can number' around the throne of God in heaven.

For reflection

A prayer

Heavenly Father, we give you thanks and praise for all those who have gone before us in the faith of Christ. As we honour their memory and rejoice in their fellowship, may we be so strengthened by their example that with them we may come to share in the joys of your eternal kingdom.

Now concerning love of the brothers and sisters, you do not need to have anyone write to you, for you yourselves have been taught by God to love one another; and indeed you do love all the brothers and sisters throughout Macedonia ... But we do not want you to be uninformed, brothers and sisters, about those who have died, so that you may not grieve as others do who have no hope. For since we believe that Jesus died and rose again, even so, through Jesus, God will bring with him those who have died. For this we declare to you by the word of the Lord, that we who are alive, who are left until the coming of the Lord, will by no means precede those who have died. For the Lord himself, with a cry of command, with the archangel's call and with the sound of God's trumpet, will descend from heaven, and the dead in Christ will rise first. Then we who are alive, who are left, will be caught up in the clouds together with them to meet the Lord in the air; and so we will be with the Lord forever.

1 Thessalonians 4.9–10; 13–17

3

FOOD FOR THE JOURNEY

The Eucharist

'Eucharist' is one of four biblical names for the universally celebrated ordinance which Jesus instituted on the evening of his betrayal. The others are 'the breaking of bread', 'the Lord's Supper' and 'Holy Communion'. Each emphasizes a slightly different aspect of the service. 'Breaking of bread' takes us back to the supper at Emmaus, when Jesus was revealed to the startled disciples who lived there 'in the breaking of the bread' (Luke 24.33). 'The Lord's Supper' reflects its historical origin, in the Upper Room in Jerusalem, where Jesus shared the Passover meal, the *Seder*, with his disciples on the last night of his earthly life (Matthew 26.26). 'Holy Communion' emphasizes the element of 'fellowship' – the word translated as 'communion' (*koinonia)* could equally well be rendered as 'sharing' or 'fellowship'. 'Eucharist' means 'giving of thanks', and this, too, is a central element of the service (see 1 Corinthians 11.24). The other name by which the service is known – 'Mass' – has no direct biblical reference, but reminds us that those who are called to Christ's table are also 'sent' to be his servants in the world (John 20.21). The name is derived from the Latin word *'missa'*, to be 'dismissed' or 'sent out'.

From the very earliest times this service has been at the

centre of Christian life and worship. The first disciples in Jerusalem after Pentecost 'broke bread from house to house' (Acts 2.46) and it is taken for granted all through the writings of the apostles that on the 'Lord's Day' (Sunday, the day of the resurrection) the believers would meet for the Eucharist.

St Paul gives a vivid description of such occasions in his letter to the church at Corinth. Its context is a lengthy rebuke for the way people there were approaching the service. Some, he said, were getting drunk (presumably at the fellowship meal, the *agape*, which preceded the breaking of bread). Some ate too much and some went short. Not only that, but the apostle was concerned that some were receiving the sacrament 'in an unworthy manner', which was putting them under the judgment of the Lord.

This account in 1 Corinthians 11.20–32 is not only fascinating for the picture it gives of worship in the church a mere thirty years or so after the crucifixion, but also as the earliest record we have of the institution of the Lord's Supper. It would be a decade before the first Gospel, Mark, would provide another account of it.

In apostolic times, and for the generations that immediately followed, the breaking of bread was the occasion for the whole church in an area – a city or region, perhaps – to come together for worship. The local bishop or presbyter (elder) would preside and the deacons would distribute the consecrated bread and wine, first to the congregation and then, leaving the gathering, to Christians who were ill and housebound.

Although there was no authorized or published common liturgy, the service always followed the same pattern, one with which modern Christians will also be familiar. There would be singing, the reading of Scripture, a homily and prayers. Then the 'peace' would be shared – a 'kiss' was what Paul enjoined four times (e.g. Romans 16.16), a command endorsed by St Peter (1 Peter 5.14) – and the great prayer of thanksgiving would follow. This assumed a common shape quite early in the life of the Church, but always had at its heart the words that Jesus spoke in the upper room: 'This is my body ... This is my blood of the new covenant'. The bread and wine were distributed and shared and then, after a final song of praise, the disciples left – most of them to go to their daily work, Sunday being a normal working day.

In the nature of things, this simple liturgical shape tended over the centuries to become more and more complex, as various elements were added. The service assumed a distinct and unalterable form, while preserving the essential elements as they had been handed down by the apostles. Various doctrinal interpretations were introduced, sometimes it seems, attempts to define the indefinable: the 'Real Presence', transubstantiation, reservation of the sacrament and benediction (the use of the consecrated bread as an object of worship and blessing). These elements were present both in the Western Church (which looked to Rome as its centre of authority) and the Eastern Church, which recognized the leadership of the patriarch of Constantinople.

It was not until the first stirrings of the Reformation that anyone seriously challenged this understanding of the sacrament. The fact is, however, that since the time of the Reformation all the Churches, including the Roman Catholics, have sought to re-examine their understanding of this central rite of the faith. On the whole, this has led to simplification, so that today most of the Churches which have a recognized liturgy follow almost exactly the same pattern. Roman Catholics, Lutherans, Anglicans and Methodists, and many of the Free Churches, have looked back to the early liturgies of the Church for guidance in shaping their Eucharistic worship.

In all churches the fundamental ingredients are the same: repentance and forgiveness, the reading and preaching of Scripture, intercessory prayer, songs of worship and praise, the shared 'peace'. All centre the service around the 'Eucharistic Prayer', the Church's great act of thanksgiving for the saving action of God in Jesus. And in all of them the bread and wine are then taken and shared, before the people are 'sent out' to love and serve God in the world.

It is hard to imagine the life of Christian discipleship without this sacrament – indeed, to ignore it would be to disobey one of the most explicit commands of Jesus: 'Do this in remembrance of me' (1 Corinthians 11.24–25).

Perhaps the best clue to the meaning and purpose of this simple rite lies in those very words. Do this in *remembrance*. They take us back a thousand years before Christ, to the time of the Passover, when the Jews were to eat a meal 'in haste' before their remarkable release from slavery in Egypt. They were told to repeat this meal every year in remembrance of what God had done for them on that occasion, and today, all over the world, Jews still celebrate the Passover and remember how God brought 'us' out of Egypt. In 'remembering' (and the idea is explicit in both the Hebrew and Greek words used for it in the Bible) they are bringing the past into the present, making what God did once for all long ago in Egypt a present reality in their own lives.

That is precisely what Christians do in the Eucharist. They take the unrepeatable, once for all, sacrifice of Jesus, made at Calvary nearly two thousand years ago, and make it a present reality in their lives now. The past is brought into the present in order to transform it.

But this wonderful rite has another treasure to offer. Just as God fed those wandering Jews in the wilderness on their long pilgrimage to the Promised Land, so he feeds the people of the new covenant on their long pilgrimage of faith. We don't simply look at the sacred elements, the bread and the wine. *We eat and drink them.*

We make them part of us. We use them as nourishment on our pilgrimage, food for the journey. Jesus said, 'My flesh is true food and my blood is true drink' (John 6.55). He was not advocating cannibalism, but using vivid, even shocking language, to drive home the message. Sacramentally, spiritually, the people of God feed on him in the Eucharist.

'You are what you eat' is a modern slogan, but it embodies a basic truth. Christians, too, 'are what they eat'. It isn't necessary to hold a doctrine of transubstantiation to believe that as we obey his command, and as we 'remember' in a dynamic and life-changing way what he has done for us, Jesus feeds us with himself. He is, indeed, the 'bread of heaven', the 'living bread' that gives and sustains our lives.

For reflection

The most common names for this service serve to illustrate the many facets of its meaning for us.

The breaking of bread

This is the oldest name used for it among Christians (see Acts 2.41, where it is one of the four marks of the life of the earliest Christian community). It refers back, of course, to the fact that at the Last Supper on the night of his betrayal Jesus took bread and broke it, describing it as his 'body which is given for you'. This title emphasizes both the corporate nature of the sacrament and its close connection with the death of Jesus 'for us'. St Paul brings the two ideas together in one statement: 'The bread that we break, is it not a sharing in the body of Christ? Because there is one bread, we who are many are one body, for we all partake of the one bread' (1 Corinthians 10.16).

The Lord's Supper

This title is used in a stinging rebuke by the apostle Paul. 'When you come together, it is not really to eat the Lord's supper' (1 Corinthians 11.20) – they were more concerned to eat their own, apparently indifferent to their fellow Christians who might go hungry. However, it does emphasize a truth it is all too easy to forget when tradition and form take over – this is meant to be a *meal*. We gather at the invitation of Jesus at his table, and we share there the bread and wine – staple elements of a normal meal at the time – but do it 'in remembrance of him'.

In fact the usual format of the service emphasizes this aspect of the sacrament. We gather, we greet, we express our regret for anything that has marred our friendship with our Host or with one another. We converse: he with us, in the Bible readings and the sermon; we with him in the intercessions. Then, having made our peace with each other and with him, we come to the table, where thanks are given for the food and drink (we 'say grace'), the reason for our gathering is recalled, and then we share the meal together. Finally, very often, we then do the washing-up!

Holy Communion

The word 'communion' (found, for example, in 1 Corinthians 10.16, though more often translated 'fellowship') expresses the truth that when we join together at the Lord's Table we are in 'communion' (fellowship) with our Lord and with each other. This is the supreme outward sign of the inner and essential unity of the body of Christ, the Church. It is also why it is inconsistent, to say the least, to come to this fellowship of love and sharing in an attitude of discord with another believer. Such differences should have been confessed, repented and put right before we presented ourselves at the Lord's Table.

Eucharist

This title is also very old, going back to one of the essential elements of the sacrament, thanksgiving ('Eucharist' is simply the Greek word for thanksgiving). At the Last Supper Jesus took the bread and 'gave thanks', and every time we break bread in memory of him we do the same. At the heart of the service from earliest times has been the great prayer of thanksgiving, the 'Eucharistic prayer', in which the saving acts of God through Jesus are recalled with humility and gratitude.

The Mass

This is the title by which Roman Catholics traditionally know this sacrament. It is a corruption of the final word of the Latin mass, which sent the people of God out to go and serve him (it's based on the Latin word for 'sent'). It inevitably recalls the words of Jesus to his disciples after the resurrection: 'As the Father sent me, so I am sending you' (John 20.21), and it is perfectly captured in one of the post-communion prayers in the Church of England's liturgy: 'Send us out in the power of your Spirit to live and work to your praise and glory'. The Eucharist is not so much a divine pat on the back as a loving kick rather lower!

4

THE DOUBLE CURE

Confession and absolution

Everybody is familiar with the traditional trappings of the Catholic confessional – the box, the priest behind a grille, the anxious penitent being cross-examined about their current sins. It's been the stuff of a hundred film plots and television plays, but in fact over the last forty years the way in which confessions are heard in the Roman Catholic Church has tended to move away from boxes and grilles to a more pastoral and personal approach. But although the detail has changed (and fewer Catholics feel it necessary to go regularly to confession), the principle of private confession to a priest, followed by absolution, is still central to what is now called the Sacrament of Reconciliation – reconciliation, that is, between the sinful Christian and a holy God.

This kind of confession has been practised since the early centuries of the Church, and became linked with the idea of penance (a penalty imposed on the penitent). However, it was not until the thirteenth century that the practice of private confession to a priest followed by absolution and some simple requirement to indicate true penitence became regularized. That, with various changes of emphasis and style, is more or less the general practice of Roman Catholics today.

The Reformers were for the most part sceptical about private confession, largely because of various abuses which had crept in during the Middle Ages. It also seemed to detract from the concept of the believer's free access to God through Jesus Christ, which was a cornerstone of Reformation thinking. 'No priest but Christ!' called the Protestants, fearing a powerful priestly 'caste' would assume control over the most private and intimate areas of people's lives. Consequently the practice of 'auricular confession' (confession to a priest) virtually died out in the great Churches of the Reformation.

However, there seems to be something in human nature that at times requires the opportunity to unburden ourselves to another, and that is as true in the area of moral failure or sin as any other. In the New Testament, James urged his readers to 'confess your sins to one another, and pray for one another' (5.16). There have been movements which have attempted this practice in modern times, but it is, of course, fraught with problems and dangers. The exhibitionist is tempted to attract attention by 'confessing' a catalogue of colourful sins; the introvert is intimidated by the pressure to 'come out with it', while others may in fact be led into temptation by what they hear. It may have worked well in the close and disciplined atmosphere of a church in the first century, but the general view now would be that it is not likely to be helpful.

The Church of England long ago recognized in its Book of Common Prayer that there might be those who were unable to quieten their consciences by making confession privately or even in a 'general confession' in church. For such it advised that they should seek out a 'godly and learned minister of God's Word' in whose presence they could make their confession and be assured, on the authority of Scripture and the promise of God, that they were indeed forgiven and absolved.

In fact, there can be few Christian ministers of any

tradition who have not been approached by members of their congregations with some similar request. It surprised me, in my first parish – a church with a clear evangelical tradition – to find that I was in fact 'hearing confessions' quite regularly. Neither I nor they tended to call it that, but that was what it was – an anxious, sometimes guilt-ridden Christian seeking an assurance that a sin confessed and repented was truly forgiven. My style was to keep the whole thing formal, always to do it in church (not a cosy chat in the vicarage), and to discourage any tendency to go into details about the particular sin being repented. Of course I stressed that what they were saying they were saying to God, though in my presence, and that there was an unconditional assurance of total confidentiality about the whole occasion. I can say that for several people this experience was truly life-changing.

Over the years the Church of England has adopted a simple mantra about private confession: 'All may, none must, some should'. I feel that is a fair statement of the position. The role of the Christian minister is to be there for the people before God, and to be there for God before the people. To embrace in that equation the undoubted anxieties of some about their sins and failures, and to represent to them the absolute assurance that what is repented is forgiven for ever, is simply to do what the minister is called to do. And for the people of God, there is great comfort in the thought that there is a human ear, a human voice, a human heart that is with them as they stand before God in all their weakness, failure and shame.

For reflection

Therefore confess your sins to one another, and pray for one another, so that you may be healed. The prayer of the righteous is powerful and effective.

James 5.16

Let the water and the blood
From thy riven side which flowed,
Be of sin the double cure:
Cleanse me from its guilt and power.

A. M. Toplady

Our brother has been given to us to help us. He hears the confession of our sins in Christ's stead, and he forgives our sins in Christ's name.

Dietrich Bonhoeffer

5

THE CLOUD OF
WITNESSES

Learning from the saints

According to the New Testament, *all* Christians are 'saints'. That doesn't mean that in the everyday sense of the word they are 'saintly', nor that they lead lives of unblemished holiness, but simply that God's purpose for them is holiness. They are 'called to be saints' (Romans 1.7), it's the direction in which they are moving.

Over the centuries the Church has recognized in some of its members particular or unmistakable signs of that 'holiness'. In the earliest centuries this usually involved martyrdom. Those who died for the sake of Christ were revered. They would have a place of honour in heaven (Revelation 7.14–17). Alongside them would be Christ's servants, the prophets, and 'saints and all who fear his name' (Revelation 11.18). Yes, there will be in John's vision a 'vast multitude which no one could number' before that heavenly throne, but that did not preclude a special honour for those whose Christian discipleship had been an inspiration and blessing to many.

It's easy to feel rather ambivalent about this notion of 'special honour'. Are not all who are 'in Christ' equal before the throne of God? The answer is undoubtedly 'yes' –

equally accepted, equally cherished, equally inheritors of the kingdom of heaven. But the saints and martyrs (in this special sense) are there to continue to inspire and encourage those of us still struggling to be faithful Christians on earth.

They are, one assumes, the 'cloud of witnesses' (literally, 'martyrs') spoken of by the writer of the letter to the Hebrews (12.1). Their 'witness' continues to challenge us. Without their example of faith (and the same writer spends the whole of his chapter eleven listing examples from the Old Testament), we might be tempted to think that the task is too great, the battle too hard, the prize too elusive. Yet there they stand, the 'noble army of saints and martyrs', to remind us that Jesus never said it would be easy, but that he would be with his people 'to the end of the age' (Matthew 28.20).

It's sometimes claimed that the Pope 'makes saints'. Of course, he doesn't. God makes saints; holiness is a work of the Holy Spirit. What the Pope does do is *recognize* in some Christians marks of exceptional saintliness – usually people already marked out by their lives and their achievements. However, we don't have to subscribe to the rather complicated process by which the Roman Catholic Church raises some Christians to beatification and then to canonization (a place in the Church's Calendar of saints) in order to honour those who have gone before us and left us examples of faith and holiness.

The writer of the letter to the Hebrews certainly saw the role of the great heroes of faith from the past in building up our faith in the present. He runs through a long catalogue of noble figures from the Hebrew Scriptures, using each to illustrate some aspect or other of godliness, courage and faith. His account culminates in a crescendo of admiration: 'They were stoned to death, they were sawn in two, they were killed by the sword; they went about in skins of sheep and goats, destitute, persecuted, tormented – of whom the world was not worthy.' These 'saints' of the Old Testament were to be 'commended for their faith', yet they did not 'receive what was promised'. God had 'provided something better' so that eventually, with the saints of the new covenant, they would be 'made perfect'.

From there, the writer goes on to speak of that 'great cloud of witnesses' who surround the Christian believers – presumably both the saints of faith from the Old Testament and the martyrs of the Christian era. Inspired by their presence, he urges his readers to pursue the path of Christian discipleship with total commitment, laying aside everything that could hinder and 'looking to Jesus, the pioneer and perfecter of our faith' (12.2).

In these passages, it seems to me, we have a balanced and positive picture of the role of the 'saints' in the life of the Christian. It is a matter of example, encouragement, inspiration and motivation. We can, in a way, identify with them because like us they were fallible human beings. Yet they show us what God can do with an 'ordinary' human life dedicated to him. They are accessible models of lives lived in the power of the Holy Spirit.

We can learn from Francis and Clare the value of a life freed from slavery to possessions. We can learn from Augustine of Hippo the converting power of repentance and faith. We can learn from the mother of Jesus the sheer simplicity of obedience: 'I am the Lord's servant. Let it be with me according to your word.' Reflecting on the lives of those who have gone before us on the pilgrimage of faith can transform the way we live our Christian lives.

For reflection

Therefore, since we are surrounded by so great a cloud of witnesses, let us also lay aside every weight and the sin that clings so closely, and let us run with perseverance the race that is set before us, looking to Jesus the pioneer and perfecter of our faith.

Hebrews 12.1–2

In God, and in his Church, there is no difference between living and dead, and all are one in the love of the Father. Even the generations yet to be born are part of this one divine humanity.

Sergius Bulgarov

Saints are persons who make it easier for others to believe in God.

Nathan Soderblom

6

THE LORD'S SERVANT

Honouring Mary

Among the Calendar of saints honoured by Christians down the centuries, it's obvious that one figure stands out above all the others – Mary, the mother of Jesus. More churches are dedicated to her, more shrines have been built in her honour, more people have been baptized with her name, more petitions and supplications have been addressed to her than any other figure in Christian history. Indeed, there was a time in the Middle Ages when it almost seemed that Christianity was in fact the religion of Mary and that the Holy Trinity had a fourth member, the one often called 'the mother of God'.

There are many explanations offered for this astonishing fascination (one might almost say obsession) with the humble woman from Nazareth who accepted the awesome responsibility of bearing the child who was the Son of God. It goes without saying that no one in the history of our race had been given a more honoured role, yet it was one that would bring her enormous pain and sorrow, as well as joy and fulfillment. However, the New Testament is restrained in its treatment of Mary – John's Gospel does not mention her once by name, always referring to her as 'the mother of Jesus'. There is no suggestion either in the letters of Paul, Peter and John nor in the writings of the Fathers of the Church in the first two centuries that she was other than a faithful, obedient woman whose life was a model of humility and faith. Later centuries saw the gradual elevation of Mary from her role as 'mother of Jesus' to her common title in the Greek Church, *theotokos* (bearer of God), to the more questionable 'Mother of God' familiar to us through prayers like the 'Hail Mary'. Logically, the 'Mother of God' would herself be God – the first cause of the first cause, as it were!

Arguments about such questions do nothing to further a balanced, positive and spiritually helpful devotion to Mary. I remember a young student telling me many years ago that he found contemplating the purity of Mary a tremendous help in his own struggle for purity. For others, her humble acceptance of responsibility is a model for every Christian, while for some the joyful words of the *Magnificat* – 'My soul magnifies the Lord and my spirit rejoices in God my Saviour' – captures perfectly the spirit of gratitude in worship. Some draw inspiration from the sorrowing figure at the cross, the universal Mother mourning for her son. And what can we make of the moment when, in the upper room, she met the same Son risen, though not yet ascended? If the Middle Ages might be accused of offering excessive adoration to this remarkable woman, then it's equally true that Christians in the Reformed tradition have culpably tended to freeze her out of their language of prayer and praise.

Jesus was 'born of Mary'. We confess that in the Creeds, we sing it in our hymns, we know it from our Bibles. It was Mary who taught the infant Jesus his prayers, told him the stories of the great heroes of the faith, took him to synagogue and – memorably – to the Temple in Jerusalem. She prepared his meals, called him in from the streets of Nazareth when it was bed time. Humanly speaking, no one did more to shape Jesus as a person than Mary; it was indeed the role and responsibility of the Jewish mother. Clearly, some of the things he later did mystified her and troubled her spirit, but the mother became the disciple, none the less, and following him to Jerusalem with the other women eventually stood by the cross on that bleak and sunless afternoon.

It isn't hard to honour this woman, nor to learn from her quiet but determined faith. When she was chosen for her role, the divine master plan for our redemption required just such a woman – self-effacing, modest, obedient, wise. She was the essential link between the human and the divine, a woman in whose womb was cradled for nine months the divine Son of God. However we understand the mystery of the conception of Jesus, Mary was the chosen instrument of the divine purpose. The Saviour of the world was a foetus within her before he was a baby in her arms and a young man striding the lanes of Galilee. To honour her is to honour him.

Some people, of course, address prayers to Mary. In fact, there is probably no prayer other than the Lord's Prayer which is more regularly spoken than the Hail Mary, in which she is invited to 'pray for us sinners'. I doubt whether envy or resentment is a common condition in heaven and it is hard to believe that the Father or the Son would take offence at prayers addressed to her, even though the New Testament seems quite clear that Christian prayer is addressed in the Spirit, through the Son, to the Father. However, it is hard to resist the feeling that Mary herself would have none of it. 'Do whatever he tells you,' she told the servants at the wedding in Cana (John 2.5). Like John the Baptist, her calling was to point to the Saviour, not replace him.

On the other hand, all of us from time to time surely ask people to pray for us. An awkward exam, a worrying illness, a crisis in the family: what is more natural than to ask a friend or pastor to pray for us? It's not a million miles from that to asking Mary, or another of the saints of God, to 'pray for us', provided we are quite clear that their prayers, like ours, are only effective when they reach the 'throne of grace', God himself, through the one Mediator, Jesus.

So what, in practical terms, can devotion to Mary contribute to our pilgrim journey on the well-travelled road? First, as with all the 'saints' (including the ones now living, even in our local congregations), we can take encouragement and inspiration from her example. We can be strengthened and encouraged by her simple but strong faith in God. Like her, we can be ready for the voice of God that calls us to serve him or to be a part of his purposes in the life of others. We can meditate and reflect on the qualities that made her the woman she was, and seek to model them in our own lives. And we can please Jesus by honouring the one he honoured, the one who stood by him from the manger at Bethlehem to the darkness of Golgotha and the strange joy of the resurrection. We can, with absolute faithfulness to the Scripture, join with the angel Gabriel in saying, 'Hail Mary, full of grace. The Lord is with you! Blessed are you among women.'

For reflection

The angel came in unto her and said, 'Hail, thou that art highly favoured, the Lord is with thee: blessed art thou among women.' And when she saw him, Mary was troubled at his saying, and cast in her mind what manner of salutation this should be. And the angel said unto her, 'Fear not, Mary; for thou hast found favour with God.'... And Mary said, 'Behold the handmaid of the Lord; be it unto me according to thy word.'

Luke 1.28, 29.38 (KJV)

Mary's humble acceptance of the divine will is the starting point of the story of the redemption for the human race from sin.

Alan Richardson

The feast we call *Annunciato Mariae*, when the angel came to Mary and brought her the message from God, may be fitly called the Feast of Christ's Humanity, for then began our deliverance.

Martin Luther

7

SELF-DENIAL

Fasting and personal discipline

Perhaps because eating and drinking are so absolutely fundamental to our existence, abstaining from them for periods of time has always been seen as a way of exercising personal discipline – 'keeping the body under', in the language of St Paul. Fasting is common to almost every religion and was an important element in Jewish practice from early times. Jesus mocked the people who made a show of their fasting, covering their heads with ashes, wearing a dismal look on their faces and appropriately sombre clothes on their backs. 'Truly I tell you,' he said, 'they have received their reward' – presumably, public respect and admiration for their piety. When his followers fasted, they should 'put oil on your head and wash your face, so that your fasting may be seen not by others but by your Father who is in secret' (Matthew 6.16–18).

For Jesus, then, and for Christians since, fasting is a commendable exercise in spiritual discipline, to be decided on and carried out by the disciple privately. There were times when fasting seemed more appropriate. Jesus himself fasted during his temptation in the wilderness (Matthew 4.2). The apostle Paul fasted before his baptism (Acts 9.9), a practice which became common in the early centuries of the Church. Fasting was also practised as a sign of deep commitment in prayer (Acts 13.2) – when Paul and Barnabas appointed elders (presbyters) for the churches they had planted they 'entrusted them to the Lord with prayer and fasting' (Acts 14.23).

Fasting is almost always in the Bible seen as part of prayer, or an evidence of humility and repentance at times of turning to God. Indeed, the Old Testament prophets saw fasting without repentance as an empty exercise (see, for example, Jeremiah 14.12). When the Christian Church adopted fasting as part of its way of life, it was usually employed as a penitential preparation for days of celebration, Lent being the most obvious example. Before that Fridays (being the day of the crucifixion) and Wednesdays were also observed as days for fasting.

At first fasting meant complete abstinence from food during the whole or part of the fast day. Later some fasts simply involved a restricted diet. The Eastern churches observed the days of fasting with greater strictness, and they still do; they also have many more of them. In the Western Church Lent and Fridays were observed more or less universally, though with decreasing strictness as the centuries passed. The Roman Catholic Church now has only two binding fast days, Ash Wednesday and Good Friday, but Christians generally regard Lent as a time of serious self-examination and reflection, which for most includes some kind of regime of self-denial or personal discipline.

People talk of 'giving up something for Lent', typically smoking or chocolate! In fact the true principle of fasting is more concerned with our 'taking on' something for Lent: more time for prayer, a determination to read the Bible or a devotional book, or a resolution to attend a mid-week service regularly. Alongside that, however, can well go a degree of abstinence, to give authenticity to our protestations of repentance. Hunger may not automatically fuel devotion, but a full stomach and a glass or two of wine can very effectively put out its fire.

Of course, fasting, like any other spiritual discipline, can be carried to excess, and there are many examples from the early centuries of the Church onwards of people who have taken it to dangerous and occasionally fatal extremes. It is crystal clear from the teaching and practice of Jesus and the apostles that there is nothing intrinsically wrong with enjoying our food and drink. They are gifts of God. It's no accident that at the heart of Judaeo-Christian worship are two meals, the Passover and the Eucharist. The early Church's 'love-feast', the *agape*, was a celebration of the most profound fellowship. The culmination of the awesome picture of the fulfilled purpose of God in the book of Revelation is the 'wedding-banquet of the Lamb'. It is *because* food and drink, and the company with which we share them, are so central to what we are as human beings that fasting is valuable as a sign of discipline, not *despite* it.

Fasting is not by any means the only way in which the Christian can seek to shape his or her life more responsibly. Many people have found that stewardship of our time is also a kind of fasting. It's sometimes a salutary exercise to keep a timetable of our daily activities to see how much of our time is wasted or spent on fruitless or pointless activities. People say that they have 'no time' to pray, or to go to church regularly. What they actually mean is that they prefer to use the time they have on other things. After all, the average adult Briton spends 27 hours a week watching television. A round of golf takes about three hours. A visit to the hairdresser may well take a woman three hours or more. Now none of these is *wrong*, but it is relevant to ask how we can say there is 'no time' for something as vital as prayer or worship when time is so liberally allocated to the things we enjoy doing. Frankly, we find time, or we make time, for what we truly want to do.

It is, of course, one thing to say that fasting is a 'good thing' and quite another to appreciate exactly how what is effectively starving ourselves can be the will of God. The obvious answer to that lies in the experience of millions of devout people down the ages, including, as we have seen, Jesus himself. Though that may be the 'obvious' answer, most of us would probably find greater assurance through testing its efficacy for ourselves.

Indulgence is clearly an unhelpful practice. Those who eat more than they need, or drink more than is good for them, not only endanger their physical health, they risk living in a kind of constant stupor, a style of life devoid of energy, sensitivity and grace. Moderation has always been held up as a Christian virtue, as opposed to abstinence on the one hand and indulgence on the other.

The difference between moderation (as our 'normal' lifestyle) and fasting is that from time to time, and for a specific purpose, we can voluntarily abstain from things which we enjoy in order to demonstrate that we are in control of our appetites rather than our appetites being in control of us. Strangely – and a simple trial will demonstrate the truth of this – to assert control over what is instinctive can give us a fresh sense of spiritual freedom. My body and its appetites (good and normal though they may be) will not have dominion over my mind and spirit.

In that renewed sense of freedom we may find a fresh 'appetite' for other fare: meditation, reflection, prayer, praise. Certainly prayer will be given a new authenticity, because the act of fasting demonstrates a seriousness, a sense of divine priority, which the very routine of regular prayer can tend to undermine. When our time of fasting comes to an end, we can return to our normal balanced lifestyle, perhaps with a fresh sense of gratitude for the gifts of food and drink. As the old Scottish saying goes, 'Ye never ken the wealth of water till the well gangs dry'. Those who have fasted are less likely to take for granted the joy of our 'daily bread', much less the gladness of a shared glass of wine or a warm dish of cooked food.

We may laugh at Christians in the past who squatted on poles, lived in caves, or survived for months on nothing but bread and water in order to prove their devotion. To us it was at best eccentric, at worst a total distortion of faith in a generous and gracious God who wills abundant life for his people. But if we laugh at them, might we not also weep for our contemporary generation, which seems in danger of losing any sense at all of self-discipline? Somewhere there is a balance to be struck. It cannot and must not be a choice between excessive self-denial and total self-indulgence. Those who have learnt the secret of self-discipline (and most of us are still novices at it) are those who have also learnt the secret of self-fulfillment.

For reflection

'And whenever you fast, do not look dismal, like the hypocrites, for they disfigure their faces so as to show others that they are fasting. Truly I tell you, they have received their reward. But when you fast, put oil on your head and wash your face, so that your fasting may be seen not by others but by your Father who is in secret; and your Father who sees in secret will reward you.'

Matthew 6.16–18

Self-discipline never means giving up anything, for giving up is loss. Our Lord did not ask us to give up the things of earth, but to exchange them for better things.

Fulton Sheen

8

THE SIGN OF CHRIST

Making the sign of the cross

I remember being in a village near Bethlehem many years ago. I wanted directions to the 'city of David' and asked an elderly Arab man who was standing by the road-side. He didn't speak English and I don't speak Arabic, but after some laughs and lots of gestures I managed to discover from him the way I should go. As I was about to leave, he looked at me with a question on his face, touching my elbow. I paused, and he made the sign of the cross. He was simply saying to me, 'I'm a Christian'. Although it was not then something I habitually did, I also and rather clumsily made the same sign, and we embraced.

As I drove off towards Bethlehem I thought what a powerful and moving symbol that sign is. To trace on one's forehead and chest the shape of the instrument of our redemption is a profoundly significant thing to do. We are putting ourselves, as it were, under the sign of the cross, identifying ourselves with the One who for our sake suffered and died on it. It's hard to think of any gesture we could make which would signify a deeper or more challenging commitment.

Mind you, I can recall being told of an occasion when the sign was ludicrously misinterpreted. For days a Christian who commuted on the same train every day had watched the man opposite sit down in his seat and then make the sign of the cross, as though dedicating the journey and the day to God. Eventually he felt he had to speak. 'I've noticed,' he said, 'that every day when you sit down you make the sign of the cross. I assume, then, that like me you are a Christian.' The man looked at him with some bafflement, and then grinned. 'No,' he said, demonstrating his daily routine. 'I'm simply checking glasses, tie pin, wallet and diary.'

Of course I'm aware that the sign of the cross is often made casually (a bit like the commuter with his checklist), or simply as a religious routine. For that matter, it is sometimes made in jest. Yet misuse does not make a practice invalid, any more than the existence of counterfeit bank notes invalidates the existence of genuine ones. When the sign of the cross is an outward expression of an inner conviction, it is the real thing, a simple witness to faith and a reminder to ourselves about the identity of the Lord we serve and the lengths he went to for our salvation.

Sometimes a footballer running on to the field of play will cross himself. This might be seen as no more than a superstitious invocation of divine help in winning the match. Yet I know of players who are deeply and sincerely Christian who make the sign because they want their public behaviour – not just the way they play but the way they carry themselves – to be consistent with that profession. They feel the need of God's help in that aim, and when prayer is impossible or inappropriate, this simple gesture of faith and commitment meets their need. They also know that the crowd have seen it, and that their behaviour on the pitch will, for better or worse, be taken as a test of the reality of their faith – and perhaps of the credibility of the whole Christian faith. Publicly to align ourselves with Jesus Christ in such a way is, in other words, a fearful responsibility, but at the same time a powerful incentive to 'walk the talk'.

Of course for the most part Christians use the sign of the cross either in their private prayers or in church. It usually accompanies the words 'in the Name of the Father and of the Son and of the Holy Spirit' and is therefore an act of commitment to the Holy Trinity. Many people make the sign of the cross on first waking in the morning, or before starting their night prayers. In public worship it is often used just before receiving the elements at Holy Communion, and at the words of absolution or the blessing.

For myself, as a Christian in the evangelical tradition, I have found making the sign of the cross helpful in my private life of prayer as well as from time to time in church. I find that using it sparingly, rather than constantly and perhaps rather casually crossing myself, makes it a valuable aid to concentration and commitment. It seems wholly appropriate as I wait to receive the bread and wine at the altar rail. After all, this sacrament 'proclaims the Lord's death until he comes again' (1 Corinthians 11.26). The sign of the cross places me where I ought to be, face to face with my crucified Saviour. When I am myself administering communion, I can see time and again the unobtrusive devotion of those who cross themselves as they receive. I have heard all the arguments against the practice, but truthfully can think of no conceivable reason why a Christian who finds this simple gesture helpful shouldn't do it. Equally, I can think of no valid reason why anyone who finds it difficult or distracting should feel compelled to use it. As the apostle said, 'Let everyone be fully persuaded in their own mind'.

For reflection

I saw another angel ascending from the rising of the sun, having the seal of the living God, and he called with a loud voice to the four angels who had been given power to damage earth and sea, saying, 'Do not damage the earth or the sea or the trees, until we have marked the servants of our God with a seal on their foreheads.'

Revelation 7.2–3

May I never boast of anything except the cross of our Lord Jesus Christ, by which the world has been crucified to me, and I to the world.

Galatians 6.14

9

AIDS TO DEVOTION

Icons, candles and the rest

If there is one thing that provokes the Protestant soul it is the sight of a church or shrine stuffed full of icons, candles, statues and crucifixes. I can remember my own reaction on my first visit to the Church of the Nativity in Bethlehem, where what was once a bare cave is now buried under a positive avalanche of objects of devotion. A subsequent visit to the Church of the Holy Sepulchre in Jerusalem confirmed the impression. Somewhere in the darkness, through the smoke of incense and hidden by mountains of what looked like religious tat was, apparently, the rock tomb where the Saviour was buried and from which he rose on Easter morning.

Subsequently I have learnt that such places are not necessarily typical of Catholic or Orthodox devotion (for all sorts of historical reasons), and the Second Vatican Council certainly changed the appearance of many Catholic churches. Nevertheless the impression remains that clutter clouds devotion rather than aiding it, and that the commandment warning of the sin of idolatry is sometimes in danger of being forgotten in the rush to decorate and inspire.

However, there is a vast difference between the use of icons and lights, for example, on the one hand, and what the book of Exodus calls 'graven images' on the other. Some of the Western dislike for the sort of thing we find in Bethlehem and in some churches in Jerusalem is simply a matter of taste, but there is also a genuine fear that significant borders may have been crossed between devotion and idolatry. Before condemning all such practices, however, it is surely wise to look more closely at them. After all, they have been a source of great spiritual inspiration for millions of people for nearly two thousand years.

There is no doubt that images were condemned in the second of the Ten Commandments. It could not be more explicit: 'You shall not make for yourself an idol, whether in the form of anything that is in heaven above, or that is on the earth beneath, or that is in the water under the earth' (Exodus 20.4). This was taken by the Jews as a ban on all images, whether of animals or humans, or attempted portrayals of God himself, and certainly from the time of the Maccabees in the second century BC any kinds of image were strictly banned from the Temple.

This makes it strange that from very early times – certainly the second century AD – pictures and drawings of sacred objects and people were to be found on Christian sites like the catacombs. At first many of these were symbolic – a fish, to honour the sacred titles of Jesus (the initial letters of 'Jesus Christ Son of God' in Greek spell the word 'fish'), a boat to represent the Church. However, after the period of the persecution of Christians by the Roman authorities, the images began to include pictures of baptisms and the Eucharist and then of Jesus, Mary and the apostles.

In the Eastern churches this developed into the making of icons. The word means 'image', and these pictures, usually painted in egg tempura on wood, represented Christ, the Virgin Mary or other saints, including figures from the Old Testament. As the popularity of icons increased, there was something of a reaction against them.

In the eighth century the Emperor Leo III declared all icons to be idols and ordered their destruction, and in a subsequent Synod at Hieria the veneration of icons was deemed to be heretical.

There was persecution of Christians who persisted in making and venerating icons, though eventually, at the second Council of Nicaea, these prohibitions were reversed. Even then there was a subsequent Iconoclastic Controversy in the ninth century, when again they were removed from churches, only to be reinstated forty years later.

At least these controversies show that the introduction of icons was not lightly accepted. People were aware of the danger of idolatry. The supporters of icons argued (and still do) that they are not objects of worship, but are aids to the veneration of the people they represent. The official position of the Eastern Churches is that they are means of grace when used correctly. I was fascinated to discover that Archbishop Malkhaz Songulashvili, of the Evangelical Baptist Church of Georgia, had presented a beautiful icon of St Friedswide (the patron saint of the city) to Christ Church cathedral in Oxford. Apart from anything else, I didn't know that Baptists *had* archbishops, or that icons were normally part of their devotional life.

Iain Zaczek, in his book *The Art of the Icon*, explains the clear distinction the Eastern Church makes between icons and images. 'Unlike their Western equivalents, icons were not straightforward illustrations of biblical events. Rather, they were venerated as sacred objects, spiritual tools which allowed the faithful to commune directly with God ... Artistic creativity and personal interpretation were not encouraged and indeed such notions bordered on heresy ... The laws of perspective took second place to the dictates of symbolism, and to Western eyes this has endowed icons with a primitive air that is entirely misleading' (Studio Editions, 1994).

I remember producing a programme for the BBC on the making of icons. We watched an icon maker at work and talked to him about what he saw as a sacred calling. The wood to be used is chosen long before painting begins. It is set aside, prayed over and blessed. The icon maker approaches his task rather like a preacher preparing a sermon. There is meditation and reflection on the subject, often a study of Scripture or church tradition, and many hours of prayer. Only after that does he begin to put paint to wood.

It was put to him that to paint, say, the Virgin Mary was to break the second commandment. 'No', he said, very firmly. 'I am not painting the Virgin Mary. That would indeed be idolatry. I am trying to paint *virgin-mary-ness*.' For him, the icon was a means to enable that which made Mary holy to touch the viewer and make them holy, too.

That is why icons are not 'realistic'. The figures are representative rather than descriptive. It was left to the Western Church of the second millennium to introduce realism into Christian art. Partly this was a fresh appreciation of the reality of the incarnation. Jesus was truly man and therefore had a bodily form, a likeness to which the rest of the human race can relate. Partly it was for educational reasons. With most people barely able to read, and the Scriptures offered only in Latin, the stories and teachings of the Bible were made accessible through paintings, murals, carvings and stained glass.

In all of this, the crucial difference seems to me to be between 'making images' – which could mean doing the drawings for a children's Bible – and 'bowing down and worshipping them'. It is a distinction made in the second commandment itself, made rather clearer in the NRSV's translation 'you shall not make any *idol*'. This makes the issue one of intention. If the maker's intention is to create an image for people to 'worship' – that is, to offer adoration, or to which to address prayer – then he or she is making an 'idol'. If, on the other hand, the maker intends simply to offer what we would call a visual aid, or even an aid to devotion to God or an encouragement to prayer, then what he or she makes is innocent of any notion of idolatry.

I would have to say that in my experience the borderline between the two intentions is sometimes very indistinct. Whether the artist who made a statue of the Virgin for a Catholic cathedral intended to create simply an aid to devotion to God, or knew that in practice people would kneel before it and offer prayers to Mary (which is beyond doubt 'worship') is impossible to decide, and perhaps unnecessary. It is the task of the Church to teach people the difference between that worship which is uniquely to be offered to God and the respect and reverence which may properly be paid to the noblest and holiest of his servants. Various formulae have been devised for this, but the distinctions between *latria* (the worship which is reserved for God alone), *dulia* (the worship or reverence which may be paid to the saints) and *hyperdulia* (the worship which may be offered to the Virgin Mary) can be confusing, to say the least. In practice, many Catholic Christians have simply ignored it and followed their feelings, and doubtless some of them have innocently fallen into idolatry without realizing it.

Of course many Christians in the Reformed traditions face similar questions. Thousands of Methodist homes have a bust of John Wesley prominently displayed, though few, I imagine, accord worship to it. Nevertheless, it is a 'graven image', albeit a harmless one. Many more Christians have a cross on the wall or above the bed, and increasingly, I notice, icons are popular, perhaps because people feel that they are aids to devotion, even means of grace, without inviting worship. Probably we can all be too quick to judge others in this matter – both the heresy hunter sniffing any sign of incipient worship of an object, and those who cheerfully ignore all the Bible's warnings about the dangers of idolatry.

For me, St Paul's brilliant analysis of a comparable dilemma facing the Christians at Corinth (1 Corinthians 8) is very helpful. 'We know', he says, 'that no idol in the world really exists, and that there is no God but one.' Nevertheless, for the sake of those who are worried by it, or whose consciences trouble them, he urges his flock to be very careful about their attitude to meat that has been offered to idols. They are free to eat it (because idols are nothing) but they are not free to cause a fellow-Christian to stumble.

The relevance of that to the place of paintings, statues and images in Christian devotion seems to me to be that they are 'nothing', in the sense that there is only one God and he can't be 'trapped' in a statue or image. On the other hand, all of us should be careful that this liberty doesn't lead us to lose sight of the danger of confusing the thing created by human hands with the divine Creator of everything that exists. As with so many things in the Christian life, the issue is really about intention. To whom is my true worship really directed?

None of this affects one of the most common and simple acts of Christian devotion, and one practised, I notice, right across the traditions of Christianity today. I mean the lighting of a candle. When I am on duty in the cathedral at Oxford, where I'm an honorary canon, I usually position myself near the candle-stand. During the day literally hundreds of people will pause there, take a candle and light it, and then spend a quiet moment in reflection or prayer. Sometimes, seeing me standing there, they say, 'I lit it for my sister, who's having an operation tomorrow', or 'I lit it in memory of my husband', or for a friend who is in difficulties or because there is a crisis in the family. What they are really doing is offering an inarticulate but heartfelt prayer. In an age when many have lost the language of prayer, lighting a candle is at least a way to connect our needs, our longings and hopes, to the unseen God. It is not, I think, a very long way from lighting that candle to the rediscovery of the 'art' of prayer. It was, after all, the apostle Paul himself who talked of silent prayer, expressed through sighs and groans, as the work of the Holy Spirit (Romans 8.26–27).

Similar to the lighting of a candle, but different in its intention, is the use of incense. Here we are certainly on biblical grounds, from the practice of the Temple from early times, with its 'altar of incense', to the 'golden bowls full of incense' in Revelation, which are 'the prayers of the saints' (5.8). That reference identifies the unique symbolism of incense, which rises in pungent clouds into the skies, like the words of a prayer. Its odour is 'sweet-smelling' to God, because it carries the savour of human devotion, rising before God with the prayers of his people (see Revelation 8.4).

Incense is seldom used in the churches of the Reformation, though its practice has been revived in some quarters. It's hard to see why there is such reticence about something that speaks so powerfully of the beauty of prayer and the openness of God to our petitions and worship. Certainly Christian worship can effectively use all our senses – touch, hearing, speech, sight – so why not smell? Just as a lighted candle in the middle of the room seems to invoke a spirit of worship, so perhaps a simple bowl of incense wafting its sweet odour into the air may invoke a spirit of prayer.

Not everybody will find help from the kind of aids mentioned in this chapter, and some may not wish to use them at all. But it is demonstrably true that the right environment and a helpful visual and sensual setting can create an atmosphere of prayer. Of course we can pray anywhere – on the bus, walking down the street or in a noisy and distracting room full of people. Yet even Jesus went to a 'quiet place' to pray, and he advised his disciples to do the same (Matthew 6). True prayer is in its way very demanding emotionally. It requires discipline – we are all familiar with the problem of wandering thoughts! If an icon, a candle or a picture help us to find that 'atmosphere' and achieve that discipline, then they are for us gifts of God, means of grace.

'Lord, teach us to pray', the disciples asked Jesus. Perhaps we all need to learn again the language of prayer. What seems certain is that in an age of image, colour and illustration, the children of earth can learn good lessons from the brush of the artist, the shutter of the photographer, the hands of the sculptor. We do not need or want idols, but we do need help, and their gifts offered to God may be the catalyst of spiritual renewal for many a Christian trapped in an arid wilderness of the soul.

For reflection

He is the image *(Greek: ikon)* of the invisible God, the firstborn of all creation; for in him all things in heaven and on earth were created, things visible and invisible, whether thrones or dominions or rulers or powers – all things have been created through him and for him. He himself is before all things, and in him all things hold together. He is the head of the body, the church; he is the beginning, the firstborn from the dead, so that he might come to have first place in everything. For in him all the fullness of God was pleased to dwell, and through him God was pleased to reconcile to himself all things, whether on earth or in heaven, by making peace through the blood of his cross.

Colossians 1.15–20

10

THE CHRISTIAN SEASONS

Using the Church Calendar

In some exasperation, St Paul rebuked the Christians at Galatia for 'observing special days, and months, and seasons' (4.10). Indeed, he alleged, they were being 'enslaved' by them. On the other hand, Paul himself was once 'eager to be in Jerusalem if possible on the day of Pentecost' (Acts 20.16). The contrast neatly summarizes why some Christians do, and other do not, observe the days and seasons of the Christian year – what is usually called the 'Calendar'. Some – probably most – find its pattern of story and remembrance powerful and compelling, providing a kind of shape to the passing months and years. Others are anxious that they might become 'slaves' to a system, losing their freedom to preach, pray and worship as and when they are led, on any particular aspect of Christian truth.

Carried to its extreme, the latter attitude led to the banning of Christmas under the Puritans of Cromwell's day. The former attitude, again carried to ludicrous extremes, produces anxious letters to the *Church Times* enquiring about the precise rules for the observance of the feast of St Agnes of the Seven Crossroads. Neither seems to me to do justice to the case for the Calendar.

The last meal Jesus had with his disciples before Golgotha was the Passover *Seder*. The first recorded incident in his boyhood was a memorable journey to Jerusalem for the festival of the Passover. From earliest times Christians marked such events as Easter, Pentecost and, eventually, the nativity of Jesus, which we call Christmas. Just as our daily lives are lived out against the constant changing scene of the seasons – seed-time, harvest, summer and winter – so our Christian lives are enriched by being lived out against the unfolding story of our salvation.

Of course, as with anything, the Calendar needs to be followed with intelligence and sensitivity. No congregation should be held hostage to its rules and regulations. Sometimes external events – world crises, a national or local tragedy, a bereavement in the church family – may properly take precedence. Such an event of huge national or local significance will be absorbing the concerns and demanding the prayers of the people, and it is little less than perverse in those circumstances to insist on following the liturgical formulae to the letter.

Nevertheless, on balance I am strongly in favour of the Calendar. Given the caveat about responding to events, I have never found it 'enslaving'. In fact, to preach on the readings set out in the Lectionary is profoundly liberating. I don't have to spend hours and hours wondering and praying what to preach about! There it is, and what sort of a preacher am I if I can't find something relevant and dynamic in the particular passages from the Scripture set out before me? Time and again, after an initial sinking of the heart ('there's nothing there for me to preach on'), I have turned back to the readings and on reflection and after prayer found 'the word of the Lord' for myself and for the congregation.

But the value of the Calendar goes far beyond simply the Lectionary. Every Advent, for instance, I give thanks that up and down the country – and indeed across the world – preachers and congregations alike are being forced to face the question of 'ultimate things'. It is all too easy to preach and celebrate a religion that gives us on earth a confidence in God, the peace of Christ and the daily help of the Holy Spirit, yet never or seldom looks beyond the horizon to the eternity to which the gospel constantly directs us. St Paul put it bluntly: 'If for this life only we have hoped in Christ, we are of all people most to be pitied' (1 Corinthians 15.19). Advent more or less compels us to think of what we are saying week by week in the Lord's Prayer: 'Your kingdom come'. It drives home the meaning of the words millions of people say each week at the Eucharist: 'Christ has died, Christ is risen, Christ will come again'. It demands that we extend our spiritual horizons.

It's not only at Advent that the Calendar corrects our perspectives. If we tend to think of Jesus solely as a divine being rather detached from our world and its concerns, Christmas forcibly reminds us that he was born in a stable and laid in a feeding trough. Following so closely on the heels of Advent, when we think of Christ coming in glory as the Judge of all, Christmas reminds us that Christianity is also an essentially earthy religion. It is the suffering Saviour who will be our Judge, not some remote celestial deity.

Lent speaks of the disciplines of the Christian life and our constant need for repentance and grace. Easter gloriously speaks of the triumph of life over death and light over darkness – but only after we have stood at the foot of the cross and seen what they cost the Son of God.

Pentecost reminds us that without the Spirit of God we can do nothing, but that with the Spirit's presence among us great things are possible. Each of us individually, and all of us collectively as the Church of Christ, need the constant renewing energy of the Holy Spirit if we are to be effective disciples of Jesus. This is not an optional extra for the especially pious. Far from it. 'No one', said Jesus, 'can enter the kingdom of God without being born of water and Spirit.' 'Anyone who does not have the Spirit of Christ', St Paul warns, 'does not belong to him.'

It is not only the great landmark festivals that give the Church Calendar its unique value. Trinity Sunday – something of a nightmare for some preachers! – and Epiphany, with its insistence that the revelation of Jesus is for the whole of the human race, remind us of essential elements of the faith which might otherwise be overlooked.

Then we must add in all the wonderful feast days of apostles, martyrs and saints, ancient and modern – that glorious 'cloud of witnesses' whom we have already considered. Peter, the Rock, speaks to us of the sometimes tempestuous journey to faith. Luke offers us an example of the faithful friend, as well as the gifted biographer. Paul reminds us that sometimes God simply turns lives around, and that we should never think of anyone as 'beyond salvation'. Then there is Francis, the messenger of godly poverty, and Julian of Norwich, with her visions of the mother-heart of God. How much poorer our faith would be without the example and inspiration of people like these.

How churches and individuals use the Calendar is very much a matter of preference, but the experience of moving seamlessly through the seasons of the Christian year, as we do with the seasons of spring, summer, autumn, winter, can be wonderfully liberating. Fresh aspects of the great story of redemption may emerge for us, new emotions may be touched and unexpected insights into the great truths of the faith, and of God's ways with us, may be discovered. The penitential seasons of Lent and Advent will ground our discipleship in the reality of human need and sinfulness. The celebratory seasons will lift up our hearts, as we give thanks for the incarnation, the resurrection and the outpouring of the Holy Spirit. Less high-profile festivals, like Epiphany and Trinity, will remind us of vital truths we might otherwise overlook.

And then, as we have seen, there are the saints and martyrs! As we remember with thanksgiving those who have gone before us, this motley army gathered now in glory can stand as examples for us, as inspiration for the daily challenges to faith. These, after all, are fellow-pilgrims with us. The only difference is that they have reached the goal towards which, in St Paul's phrase, we still press on.

No longer are the ranks of those honoured in this special way by the Church restricted to people from the distant past, from a culture and world very different from our own. For here are more recent heroes of the faith, too – Janani Luwum, who stood up to the brutal dictator Idi Amin in Uganda; Oscar Romero, murdered in his own cathedral for supporting the poor and weak in San Salvador; and Gladys Aylward, the former house-maid who led hundreds of Chinese children to safety over the hills during the Japanese invasion of their land. It is a cold heart that cannot be stirred by their stories and inspired by their example.

For reflection

As long as the earth endures, seedtime and harvest, cold and heat, summer and winter, day and night, shall not cease.

Genesis 8.22

A prayer

O God, by whose command the order of time runs its course:
forgive our restlessness, perfect our faith and, while we await the fulfillment of your promise, grant us to have a good hope through the Word made flesh,
even Jesus Christ our Lord.

(From Celebrating Common Prayer)

O God, the protector of all who trust in you,
without whom nothing is strong, nothing is holy;
increase and multiply upon us your mercy;
that with you as our ruler and guide
we may so pass through things temporal
that we lose not our hold on things eternal;
grant this, heavenly Father,
for our Lord Jesus Christ's sake,
who is alive and reigns with you
in the unity of the Holy Spirit,
one God, now and for ever.

(Collect, Fourth Sunday after Trinity)

I I

THE DAILY OFFICE

Giving shape to our quiet times

When I made an adult commitment of faith in Christ as a student I remember being taken on one side by a well-meaning counsellor and given a few rules for daily Christian living. Foremost among them was something he called the 'quiet time'. This, he explained, should include Bible reading and reflection, thanksgiving and prayer – and it ought to last at least fifteen minutes, presumably to show that I was serious about it. I took him at his word and for many, many years that was the shape of my private devotional life.

It was, in many ways, tremendously helpful. It drove me back to the Scripture, every day, and asked me not just to read it but to reflect on it seriously. It made me consider the generosity of God, who for such a slender faith had given me so many rich blessings. And it invited me to pray – for people, for situations, for the Church's mission and ministry in the world.

However, I was also aware of certain drawbacks, or rather short-comings, to this style of devotional life. Although I would have said that it was spontaneous and free, in fact I worked to a pretty strict regime, often using the same language and repeating almost word for word the same prayers. My Bible reading – following various schemes and systems – did not help me to read the Bible consecutively or in its broad context, but to read what it called 'passages', which were often, I discovered, simply the 'best bits', or the compilers' favourite proof texts for this or that theological supposition.

I knew that my prayer life needed refreshing, but it wasn't until I found the 'Daily Office', and its various parallels in other books of liturgy, that I discovered what it was I had been missing.

I knew already the value of that daily time of 'quiet'. It's what the psalmist called 'waiting on God', which sounds very passive but is in fact a dynamic experience of hope and trust. In this biblical kind of 'waiting' we are alert, attentive to God – the psalmist's picture is of a servant 'waiting' for a signal or command from his or her master. Another of the images from the Psalms is of the watchmen on the walls 'waiting' for the dawn, so that they can wake the city. These are not by any means passive images: woe betide the watchman, or the servant, who fell asleep on the job! In the devotional oasis which is the Christian's 'quiet time' (whatever we call it), our spiritual nerves are tuned, our spiritual ears are open, our feet and hands are ready to respond. As we open the Scriptures, as we reflect and pray, so essential communication takes place between the believer and the one in whom he or she believes.

All of that I knew, in a way, already. But what had happened was that the very process had become stuck. Now it may well be that people who have grown up with a daily office and liturgical prayer also get stuck (and if so it may be that a few months of unstructured spontaneity in prayer would 'unstick' them!). For me, however – and I find the experience is not uncommon – what should have been spontaneous and unstructured was in fact as set in a routine as any liturgy could ever be.

The discovery of the Daily Office was a revelation. Whether one uses the Common Worship 'Daily Prayer', or the Franciscan 'Celebrating Common Prayer', or the Iona or other equivalents, is unimportant. It is the balanced diet of psalmody (the prayer language of Jesus himself), readings from the Scriptures, and a treasury of praise and prayer from traditions old and new – with plenty of room for spontaneous prayer built into it – which nourishes the spirit and creates a kind of spiritual highway over which God can communicate with us, and we with him. It is not the length – most of these forms would take someone on their own no more than fifteen minutes a day – but the discipline, the shape, the balance and the feeling of drawing water from a very deep well of spirituality, past and present, which is so rewarding.

One of the troubles I used to find was that I felt I needed to be 'in the mood' for a 'quiet time', and that if I wasn't, for any reason, it was a failure. The advantage of the 'Office' is that it is designed, and only really works properly, for use at more or less the same time of day every day. Some people observe several 'Offices' during the day, often at the old monastic times – lauds, nones, matins, compline and so on. But even to have one sacred moment, guarded as well as it is possible to do in the rush and bustle of modern life, is in itself a blessing. For that moment no 'mood' is needed. It is a rendezvous with the Creator. As the familiar opening words are spoken, we are led firmly into his Presence, and the seriousness of the business we are about should be enough to hold us attentive and responsive. Is it really possible to say 'In the Name of the Father, and of the Son, and of the Holy Spirit' and *not* be conscious that we are about heavenly work?

I would not decry any serious discipline of daily prayer and Bible reading. I admire, and have used, several of the excellent daily Bible reading schemes that are on the market. I know the danger of 'vain repetition'. Yet I also know that for many Christians the old path of praying with the Daily Office is one that leads into the divine presence time and time again. What more could one ask?

Some daily prayers

Blessed are you, Sovereign God, creator of all;
To you be glory and praise for ever!
You founded the earth in the beginning
and the heavens are the work of your hands.
As we rejoice in the gift of your presence among us,
let the light of your love always shine in our hearts
and your praises be ever on our lips,
Father, Son and Holy Spirit:
Blessed be God for ever!

(Morning Prayer, Wednesdays)

Light of the world, in grace and beauty,
mirror of God's eternal face,
transparent flame of love's free duty,
you bring salvation to our race.
Now, as we see the lights of evening,
we raise our voice in hymns of praise;
worthy are you of endless blessing,
Sun of our night, lamp of our days.

(Evening Song, Tuesdays, based on an early Greek hymn)

(Both from Celebrating Common Prayer, *Society of St Francis)*

12

INWARD RELIGION

The conversion of heart and will

There's not much doubt which sin Jesus regarded as the most serious – hypocrisy. Even the swindling tax-collectors and the women of the streets, he said, would enter the kingdom of heaven before the hypocrites. They are 'play-actors' – the literal meaning of the word. They are people who play at being religious, whose religion is on the surface only. 'Outwardly,' he told some Pharisees, 'you are like white-washed tombs; inwardly you are full of corruption and death' (see Matthew 23.27). All through his ministry he sought out those who were sincere, honest, humble, even helpless – anyone except those who offered a mere show of piety.

This was a constant theme of Christ's teaching. Faced with a Samaritan woman who seemed eager to engage him in a discussion about the niceties of religious practice ('Should we worship in Jerusalem or on Mount Gerizim?') he cut the discussion short with a memorable statement about the inwardness of true religion: 'Woman, believe me, the hour is coming when you will worship the Father neither on this mountain nor in Jerusalem ... But the hour is coming, and is now here, when the true worshippers will worship the Father in spirit and truth, for the Father seeks such as these to worship him. God is spirit, and those who worship him must worship in spirit and truth' (John 4.21–24).

In the Gospels the Pharisees – possibly unfairly – have been seen as epitomizing the worst aspects of hypocrisy. Certainly Jesus denounced in fierce terms those Pharisees who made an open show of their faith while denying its fundamental principles of justice and righteousness – tithing mint, he scornfully suggested, while seizing widows' houses.

In one dialogue with some Pharisees, however, Jesus gave a revealing answer to what he seems to have taken as an honest question. They had asked him, 'When is the kingdom of God coming?' (Luke 17.20). It was a reasonable enquiry, because the message Jesus was preaching up and down the land was that the 'kingdom of God is near'. His reply was probably not at all what they expected. It emphasized the deep divide between his understanding of the kingdom of God and the popular understanding of the time. The kingdom of God is not coming with things that can be 'observed', he said. 'Nor will they say, "Look, here it is!" or "There it is!"' It is not something physical and visible, like a king on a throne or a city ringed by walls. On the contrary, he told them, it is to be seen with the inward eye of faith: 'the kingdom of God is among you'.

Much hinges on that little word 'among', which could equally well be translated as 'in' or 'within'. To decide its correct meaning, one simply has to look at its context, its place in the general flow of the argument. On those grounds, one is surely driven to the conclusion that the better translation would be 'in' or 'within'. You can't 'see' the kingdom of God in terms of rules or observations because its deepest principle is interior. The kingdom of God is not outward piety but inward faith. 'The LORD does not see as mortals see; they look on the outward appearance, but the LORD looks on the heart' (1 Samuel 16.7).

This 'inwardness' of the kingdom is a quality which, in a fascinating way, brings together both catholic and evangelical spirituality. Read the medieval mystics, sing their hymns, pray their prayers, and you find yourself in a context of profound, inner spiritual experience. 'Jesu, the very thought of thee with sweetness fills the breast!' sang St Bernard of Clairvaux in the twelfth century. 'How sweet the name of Jesus sounds in a believer's ear!' sang the evangelical parson John Newton in the eighteenth century. From what some might see as opposite ends of the theological scene, they share the same melody. Both are exulting in the inner experience of faith, the burning love of the redeemed soul for its Redeemer. It would be possible to multiply such examples over and over again.

Of course the kingdom of God has corporate significance. Christianity is not a religion of sanctified individuality. When we believe and are baptized we join a body – indeed, the Body of Christ. That body, the Church, has a common life and a common mission, which is service for the whole world. We are not born again into a vacuum, but into a family, and that family has work to do for God.

Yet the fact remains that faith is in its origin individual. We come to Christ one by one; one by one we are baptized. And the inner life of the believer is something which is personal and precious, and without it the corporate body has no living, beating heart. 'The Son of God loved *me*', exclaims St Paul, 'and gave himself for *me!*' (Galatians 2.20).

Many years ago, in the early days of my adult Christian commitment, I remember hearing an elderly bishop speaking on 'the inwardness of true religion'. His talk had a profound effect on me. It made sense of my own experience, and it made sense of so much of the Bible – the Psalms as well as the Gospels and Epistles. When the heart is conquered, then the will follows. Where heart and will agree together, then action flows. What some call the 'social gospel' works only because hearts and wills have been touched by an 'interior' experience of God himself.

Here the 'old way' has much to say to us – but so does the voice of the evangelical movement. They speak as one. We shall struggle with living a Christian life until our hearts and wills have been touched and transformed by the power and the presence of the risen Saviour. The Italian grandmother invoking the Sacred Heart of Jesus and the new convert 'asking Jesus into his heart' are at one. Inner conversion of heart and will are the building blocks of any true spirituality.

In the early thirteenth century Francis of Assisi knelt before a crucifix in the church of St Damiano and knew that his life was changed for ever. He was already a Christian, of course, but he called this his 'conversion', the great turning point in his life.

It is this experience of inner conversion, the 'turning round' of the heart and the will that shines through the lives of the saints. But it also marks out those people around us whose lives have been equally profoundly touched by the tremendous mystery of the indwelling presence of God. A former Archbishop of Cape Town, Joost de Blank, a man steeped in Catholic spirituality, wrote a book (now long out of print) on the subject of conversion. It is, he said, the transforming touch of God. He described an experience familiar to many parish priests and ministers – a woman (he suggested) in the congregation who has been a regular and faithful churchgoer for half a lifetime, but suddenly one notices a difference. The sense of routine, of duty, has been overtaken by a sense of the divine. Prayer has become real for her, worship exciting and life-changing, the Bible the dynamic voice of a living God. That, he said, is what conversion is, and that is what it does.

All of the ways of spirituality described in this book, all of the disciplines of prayer and Bible reading, the example of the saints and the grace of the sacraments will be as nothing without this inward conversion of the soul. The experience does not need to be dramatic. It need not, probably should not, follow any particular pattern or formula. It may come as a gradual realization of an irresistible inner change of heart, a deep and true repentance and a resurgence of faith. But in one way or another it is the presence of the living Christ in the centre of my life that is the foundation of faith. Upon that can be built the superstructure of spiritual discipline, of a life of prayer, of a thirst for the Scripture and a love of the means of grace. This is no 'optional extra'. This *is* the faith of the Church.

For reflection

Listen! I am standing at the door, knocking; if you hear my voice and open the door, I will come in to you and eat with you, and you with me.

Revelation 3.20

So if anyone is in Christ, there is a new creation: everything old has passed away; see, everything has become new!

2 Corinthians 5.17

I pray that, according to the riches of his glory, he may grant that you may be strengthened in your inner being with power through his Spirit, and that Christ may dwell in your hearts through faith, as you are being rooted and grounded in love.

Ephesians 3.16–17

13

THE SACRAMENT OF THE WORD

Attending to the Preacher

If you go into almost any Catholic or Orthodox church anywhere in the world, it is obvious that its central feature is the altar where communion is celebrated – though you can't actually see it in many Orthodox churches because it's behind a screen. Most of the great cathedrals of Britain, too, are clearly designed around the altar, often – in the older ones – a 'high' altar set at the top of a series of steps.

On the other hand, if you go into a Baptist, independent or congregational church, the most obvious feature is usually a large pulpit-cum-reading desk, from which the minister leads the service, reads the Scripture and preaches.

This contrast illustrates a historic difference of emphasis. From the early Middle Ages, if not earlier, the altar-table at which the Eucharist was celebrated was the focal point of the room where Christians gathered. Of course the Bible was read and sermons were preached, but these were clearly sacramental meeting places – the other essential feature was a baptistery of some kind (later a 'font'). The Protestant and evangelical movements, on the other hand, saw the reading and preaching of the Word of God as the building blocks of faith. The gospel creates the Church, they would argue, not the other way round. The priority is to teach and preach – didn't St Paul say 'Woe is me if I do not preach the gospel' (1 Corinthians 9.16)? Of course they also have a table available at which the believers can gather for the Lord's Supper, but this is seldom the focal point of the building.

As it happens, the last forty or fifty years have seen considerable changes in church design, reflecting new understandings of the importance of Scripture and preaching on the one side, and of the centrality of the Eucharist to the life of the church on the other. So in Roman Catholic churches the altar has been moved from its old position at the east end of the building, remote from the lay-people, to the nave, or even to a central position in the middle of the congregation. And in many churches in the Protestant and evangelical tradition communion is no longer an occasional 'treat' or an appendix to the main service of worship, but a service which embraces and involves the whole Christian community week by week. Consequently the communion table is often now in a more prominent position, balancing, as it were, the pulpit and lectern.

The truth is, if you want to be 'catholic' then preach the gospel (Romans 15.16), and if you want to be 'evangelical' then celebrate the Eucharist to 'proclaim the Lord's death until he comes' (1 Corinthians 11.26).

Of course, these are not two things in opposition, but the same thing done by different means. The reading and preaching of the Scripture tells the 'story' and challenges the heart and will. But the Eucharist also tells the 'story', and just as powerfully challenges the heart and the will. The first is the gospel preached, and the second is the gospel enacted.

The Church is not called to do one or the other (though it's sometimes seemed like that), but to do *both*. So 'proclaiming the Lord's death' in the breaking of bread and preaching the Word of God and listening to it, are both essential elements in Christian ministry and discipleship. Both are, in an important sense of the word, sacramental. They are outward and visible signs and means of inward and spiritual grace.

'Give attention to the public reading of scripture', St Paul urged his younger assistant Timothy (1 Timothy 4.13). In an age when many could not read at all, and others had only basic literacy skills, this was crucial. How else would they know the truth and hold fast to it? Even in our age of widespread literacy, it remains true that for many Christians their only regular interaction with the Bible is when they hear it read in church. All the more reason, of course, why it should be done really well – not rushed or gabbled, not made meaningless by wrong emphases, not entrusted to those with indistinct voices or distracting mannerisms.

Everyone who reads the Bible publicly in church should be aware that theirs is a sacred and solemn ministry – which is not the same as saying that it should be recited like a railway timetable or with an especially pious voice. Any churchgoer will recognize many failings in the public reading of scripture, just as they will be grateful for every occasion when they have heard the Bible read with intelligence, clarity and reverence.

So much for the reader – but many of the same points could be made about preachers. To be given authority by the Church to 'preach the Word of God' is an awesome responsibility, and I think most preachers are aware of that. But even here familiarity, routine, tiredness or simply a loss of spiritual vision can sometimes turn preaching into an empty and pointless pastime, in which the preacher offers the congregation 'a few thoughts about' this or that, loosely connected to one of the lectionary readings or, even worse, hung upon something in the day's newspaper or the preacher's current preoccupations. In fact, short or long, the sermon or homily is to serve the Scripture – to illuminate, apply or explain something we have just heard read aloud, to challenge and inspire the congregation in their discipleship, to focus the eternal Word of God on the needs of the people at that moment. Preaching is a God-given means by which the Scriptures can touch the hearts of particular people and change their lives.

So preaching is a sacred calling, not to be lightly undertaken. But so, in truth, is 'attending' to Scripture. The hearers, in other words, also have a responsibility; they too need to exercise a spiritual gift. The Scripture read or preached falls on human ears, but if the parable of the sower means anything it is that the crucial factor is not the quality of the seed (the Scripture, the gospel) but the nature of the soil – and the soil is the congregation, those who 'hear the Word'.

It is all too easy for members of the congregation to blame the preacher. 'I got nothing from that,' people say. Well, perhaps it wasn't an inspired or inspiring piece of oratory, or even a particularly competent exposition of the Scripture. Yet there was *something* there to nourish the spirit, so long as the preacher was using the Bible as seed and not his or her own ideas and speculations. Sometimes one feels that the congregation has decided before the preacher even begins that this is not going to be worth their close attention. It's hardly surprising, then, that they get nothing from it. Faith speaks to faith, expectation is fed. Without some degree of faith, or some expectation of nourishment, the preacher's task is likely to be a barren and unproductive affair – just like the seed that fell on stony ground in the parable of Jesus.

We the hearers are called to 'give attention' to the Word of God, to be expectant and faithful, hungry for the nourishment that it can bring. I appreciate that sometimes our hopes will be dashed and our expectations unfulfilled, but very often the fault is as much in the hearer as the preacher. Do we, for instance, regularly and humbly pray for the preacher? Do we ever express words of encouragement – and I don't mean the cursory 'Nice sermon, vicar' sort of response? Do we go home and look at the passage that has been the subject of the sermon, to find in it not only what the preacher found but also what God wants *us* to find?

If the reading and preaching of the Word of God is in any sense a sacrament, then it must be received. We are not force-fed baptism or holy communion. They are voluntarily and gratefully received. In the same way, the reading of the Scripture and its proclamation must reach our hearts and wills; we must be open to them. Perhaps, as the preacher takes the stand and prepares to preach we might pray these words: 'Lord, open your Word to my heart, and my heart to your Word.'

For reflection

But how are they to call on one in whom they have not believed? And how are they to believe in one of whom they have never heard? And how are they to hear without someone to proclaim him? And how are they to proclaim him unless they are sent? As it is written, 'How beautiful are the feet of those who bring good news!'

But not all have obeyed the good news; for Isaiah says, 'Lord, who has believed our message?' So faith comes from what is heard, and what is heard comes through the word of Christ.

Romans 10.14–17

We also constantly give thanks to God for this, that when you received the word of God that you heard from us, you accepted it not as a human word but as what it really is, God's word, which is also at work in you believers.

1 Thessalonians 2.13

'Religion is grace, and ethics is gratitude,' said Thomas Erskine. The preacher is the servant of both, and spends his life in relating the one to the other.

Donald Coggan

14

THE PATH OF TEARS

The Stations of the Cross

'Stations' are stopping places – unless, of course, it's a through train! For the last 170 years most English-speaking people have associated the word with railways, but before that its most common use was religious. 'Stations' were places where processions halted, where people stopped to pray. And the most popular of those 'stations' were undoubtedly the 'Stations of the Cross'. Almost every Roman Catholic church has its 'stations', and increasingly they are to be found in other churches too: fourteen pictures – paintings, very often – set on the wall of the church. They depict different moments on the *Via Dolorosa*, the sad path that Jesus followed on his way from the judgment hall to Golgotha, the 'Place of the Skull' – 'Calvary' in its Latin form.

Many pilgrims to Jerusalem have followed that path, as thousands do every Good Friday, and have experienced a little of what it meant in terms of suffering, exhaustion, pain and abuse. As Jesus, and the two being crucified with him, made their way through the crowds towards the place of execution outside the city walls, they would have met a barrage of noise. There was ridicule from the crowds gathered for what St Luke calls 'the spectacle'. Others felt the horror of the sight, so that there were women among the spectators who were weeping and beating their breasts. Jesus spoke to them, telling them not to weep for him, but to weep for themselves and their children, as the appalling consequences of these events were fulfilled (Luke 23.28).

The Stations of the Cross bring the images and experiences of the *Via Dolorosa* into the local church. They enable Christians on Good Friday, but also at other times, to share in some measure the lonely pilgrimage of the Saviour on his way to the cross. The pictures or engravings capture the sense of rejection as well as the physical suffering of Jesus. They remind us of the humiliation of the scourging, and of the purple robe and crown of thorns with which the soldiers set out to ridicule the one they had heard described as 'the king of the Jews'.

Some have felt that the Stations of the Cross concentrate unhelpfully on the physical suffering of Jesus, but in fact they follow, for the most part, the biblical narrative, which is restrained in its reportage of what was, by any standards, a gruesome and vicious spectacle. It took the film 'The Passion of the Christ' to turn the words of the Gospel writers into vivid, cinematic images, with the result that many people found the experience deeply shocking. Well, it *was* shocking, though the Gospels make no attempt to emphasize, much less exaggerate, the physical element of the suffering of Christ. That is left to our imaginations, filtered through our knowledge now of the *whole* story: rejection, suffering, passion, death and then resurrection. It is the story of our redemption, and at some point we have to accept that it cost Jesus, the Son of God, a hideously painful death – a *real* death, for our *real* sins.

The various Stations mark details of that long walk to destiny. Jesus takes up his cross – echoing his earlier call to his disciples to 'take up the cross daily'. To carry the cross was part of the punishment for the criminal

– to stagger to the place of execution under the weight of the cross-beam. In fact, Jesus, already weakened by the flogging he had been given, fell under its weight, and the soldiers dragged someone from the crowd to carry it. That man was Simon of Cyrene, the quintessential bystander who finds himself very much part of the action. We know little beyond his name, and a fascinating detail which Mark adds, that he was 'the father of Alexander and Rufus' (Mark 15.21). The fact that Mark, a member of the first Christian community in Jerusalem (Acts 12.12), knew this detail suggests that Simon and his family became Christians, in which case the apparently random recruitment of a man from the crowd turned out to be much more than that.

I was speaking a year or so ago at a meeting in Abingdon, in Oxfordshire, on this subject. A man in the audience related his own experience as a teenager of being in the crowd watching a Good Friday procession in Padstow in Cornwall. Suddenly one of the 'soldiers' grabbed his arm and recruited him to carry the cross. It was, he said, a profoundly moving experience, even to a young lad, and was the beginning of his own journey of faith.

There are various incidents added to the Stations for which there is no direct biblical authority – Veronica, who was said to have wiped the brow of Jesus, and various other occasions when Jesus stumbled or fell. Yet none goes beyond reasonable supposition, and all together add to our mental picture of that long and sad pilgrimage to Golgotha. This is reinforced by readings and prayers at each Station, and sometimes a hymn or song.

The Stations of the Cross go beyond being mere visual aids, like pictures in stained glass. Their very name, 'stations', tells us that they are there to be *observed* rather than simply looked at. Each station invites us to stop, to reflect, to remind ourselves of the cost of our redemption in the suffering of Jesus. In a genuine sense, by walking the Stations of the Cross we can begin to share his pilgrimage of pain. Isaac Watts' famous hymn invites us not just to 'survey' the 'wondrous cross', but to allow its image to change our whole lives. That is precisely what the Stations are meant to do as well.

For reflection

I want to know Christ and the power of his resurrection and the sharing of his sufferings by becoming like him in his death, if somehow I may attain the resurrection from the dead.

Philippians 3.10–11

(Jesus said) 'The Son of Man must undergo great suffering, and be rejected by the elders, chief priests, and scribes, and be killed, and on the third day be raised.'

Then he said to them all, 'If any want to become my followers, let them deny themselves and take up their cross daily and follow me.'

Luke 9.22–23

15

ANOINTING WITH OIL

The sign of the Spirit

I can remember watching the coronation of Queen Elizabeth in Westminster Abbey on a small black and white television back in 1953. At a very solemn moment in the proceedings the Archbishop, Geoffrey Fisher, took a spoonful of oil and anointed the new monarch's head. I had never seen an anointing before, and though I suppose I must have known that kings had been anointed with oil from early biblical times at least, I had no idea of the significance of the ceremony.

In more recent days, anointing has been used more widely in many churches, following in some cases the practice of the Roman Catholic Church, but also extending it into such areas as healing and spiritual support. Many churches have taken to anointing candidates for baptism with oil – the ancient 'chrism' and the basis of the English word 'christening'. Charismatic and evangelical Christians, as well as many others, use anointing with oil widely in healing, following the advice of the Epistle of James: 'Are any among you sick? They should call for the elders of the church and have them pray over them, anointing them with oil in the name of the Lord. The prayer of faith will save the sick, and the Lord will raise them up; and anyone who has committed sins will be forgiven' (James 5.14–15).

The first time I saw this done was in our evangelical parish church in north London in the 1950s, when a young man in our congregation contracted bone cancer. The doctors said that he should have his leg amputated at the knee, but he believed that God wanted him on both legs to serve him. Anyway, quoting this verse from James, he asked the vicar if he could be prayed for and anointed. This was duly arranged, and a number of us gathered with the vicar to carry out his wishes. None of us had ever done anything like it before, and needless to say, we had no idea what the outcome would be.

In fact, when he paid his next visit to the hospital the X-rays could detect no sign of the cancer. The plans for amputation were abandoned, he resumed normal life and was eventually ordained in the Church of England and became a highly effective evangelist. That remains the one absolutely irrefutable miracle that I have witnessed in my life.

Subsequently, I fell to thinking about the principle of anointing. What was its significance? Why had so many churches and Christians abandoned the practice completely? I was aware that anointing was a feature of the making of kings in Old Testament times (1 Kings 1.39), and discovered that it was also part of the ritual for consecrating a priest for service in the Temple (Exodus 29.7). The New Testament revealed that anointing was a way of honouring a person (Luke 7.38), and also of preparing a person's body for burial (Mark 16.1).

More than that, the promised Messiah was literally the 'anointed one' – both *messiah* and *christ* simply mean 'anointed'. So Jesus was the anointed One, a figure at once both priestly and kingly.

Clearly there was more to this practice than I had previously assumed. What did it mean to be anointed? It was obviously much more than simply the application of some oil to a person's head, hands or feet. To anoint a person, or a thing, was to set them aside for holy use. That could be anything from a stone pillar to mark a sacred place (Genesis 28.16–18), or the furnishings of the Temple (Leviticus 8.10), to the consecration of Aaron as the high priest (Exodus 29.7). In the last case, anointing seemed to carry the implication of succession, of the passing on of authority or power, as well as blessing.

This element of power and authority was also indelibly associated with the Spirit of God, both in the Hebrew and Christian Scriptures. Anointing with oil was a sign of the invocation of the Spirit of God for a particular and usually specific purpose, be it healing, ordination, consecration or blessing. It was a sacramental act, in that it had an outward and visible sign – the application of oil – and an inward grace, the meeting of a specific need. To rule as king was an awesome responsibility, which could not be discharged satisfactorily without the Spirit's grace. To minister in holy things was to involve sinful humans in what is essentially a divine activity, and hence was unthinkable without the inward grace of the Spirit. In the consecration of the high priest of Israel the blood of sacrifice was first applied, and after that the oil of blessing – only those whose sins were forgiven could receive the gift of sacred ministry (see Leviticus 8.23 and 30).

Of course, the anointing is essentially an outward sign. We can see it being applied, the recipient can feel its smoothness on his or her head, the bystanders can perhaps smell its fragrance. But the grace is inward. No amount of oil can change an unrepentant heart, or bring about any consequence that is not the will of God. Yet the sign and the thing signified are not in tension with each other, but in harmony. The believing, contrite, willing heart is 'anointed' as surely as the head, hands or feet are. Whether, in Christian terms, it is a candidate for baptism or a man or woman seeking healing of body, mind and spirit, it is their faith, their hope and trust, which receives the anointing, and in that sense the outcome depends not on the outward sign but on the inward grace.

One of the best-known examples of anointing is what used to be called 'Extreme Unction' or the 'Last Rites' – the anointing of a dying person to prepare them for the journey home to God. Since the Second Vatican Council the old names are used less commonly, and the rite is seen as simply a more focused part of the general practice of the anointing of the sick. There is still, however, something peculiarly appropriate about the anointing of a Christian at the point of death, and I have always found this simple service profoundly moving and challenging. If at any time in our lives we need the grace, presence and power of the Holy Spirit it must surely be as we embark on that final journey of faith. 'Go forth upon your journey from this world, Christian soul', the prayer begins, 'in the name of God the Father almighty who created you; in the name of Jesus Christ who suffered death for you; in the name of the Holy Spirit, who strengthens you; in communion with the blessed saints, and aided by angels and archangels, and all the armies of the heavenly host. May your portion this day be in peace and your dwelling the heavenly Jerusalem.' Usually the minister then anoints the person's forehead, hands and feet with oil. Having been present at such a rite for those very dear to me, and also having anointed members of my own congregations at the point of death, I can only say that it speaks with memorable power of the great gospel truths of forgiveness, acceptance and eternal life, at the very moment when we most need to be reminded of them.

In the modern Anglican service of baptism the priest may anoint the forehead of the candidate, with these words: 'Christ claims you for his own. Receive the sign of his cross.' Then other members of the candidate's family are invited to do the same – to dip their fingers in the oil of anointing and make the sign of the cross on the candidate's forehead. That, in essence, expresses the meaning of anointing. That which had not belonged to the Lord now belongs to him. It has been set aside, indelibly marked for divine use. Such a powerful sign will not be used lightly, but when the will of the one so marked and the intention of those making it are one it is hard to think of a more comprehensive mark of total commitment. We cannot anoint ourselves, any more than we can baptize ourselves. Human hands may apply the oil, but it is the power and grace of the Holy Spirit that makes the difference. We may wash away the oil but we can never entirely eradicate that inner anointing.

For reflection

The spirit of the Lord GOD is upon me, because the LORD has anointed me; he has sent me to bring good news to the oppressed, to bind up the brokenhearted, to proclaim liberty to the captives, and release to the prisoners; to proclaim the year of the Lord's favour, and the day of vengeance of our God; to comfort all who mourn; to provide for those who mourn in Zion – to give them a garland instead of ashes, the oil of gladness instead of mourning, the mantle of praise instead of a faint spirit.

Isaiah 61.1–3

For in him every one of God's promises is a 'Yes.' For this reason it is through him that we say the 'Amen,' to the glory of God. But it is God who establishes us with you in Christ and has anointed us, by putting his seal on us and giving us his Spirit in our hearts as a first installment.

2 Corinthians 1.20–22

16

WITHDRAW TO ADVANCE

Going on retreat

Perhaps because my father was injured in the appalling 'Retreat from Mons' in the First World War, I've always associated retreats with disaster. When I first heard the word applied to an opportunity for reflection, prayer and renewal it came as something of a surprise. Later, studying French introduced me to the saying 'recueillir pour mieux sauter' – to step back and reflect in order to make greater progress – and it began to make sense. Sometimes we all need to step back, to pause and reflect, to take stock, think and listen. When we have done so, we are in a much better position to move forward. And what is generally true in life is also specifically true of the Christian retreat.

Recent decades have seen an enormous growth in the whole retreat movement. As life has become more hectic, the pressures of time more insistent, the demands of work and family seemingly relentless, the thought of a few days free from the rat-race grows more and more appealing. For the Christian, there is the added attraction of time to reflect, meditate, read the Scriptures and pray – without being interrupted by the phone or distracted by the thought of a hundred other things that we 'ought' to be doing. To go 'on retreat', then, is far from a disastrous defeat. In fact, it is a precious, if brief, victory over the external pressures that destroy our peace of mind and undermine our attempts at a disciplined Christian life.

Our model here is Jesus himself. In the breathless language of Mark's Gospel, we read of the first full day of the public ministry of Jesus, fresh from his baptism in the river Jordan. He taught in the synagogue (1.21), he delivered a man from an 'unclean spirit' (1.25), healed Simon's mother-in-law of a fever (1.31) and then once evening had come he 'cured many who were sick with various diseases' who presented themselves at the door of the house where he was staying (1.34).

After a day like that most of us would welcome a bit of a lie-in. Jesus, however, rose 'while it was still dark' and went out to a deserted place to pray (1.35). This was to be the pattern of the rest of his life: activity, reflection, prayer – and then back to the tasks. The lakeside at Capernaum, Bethany, Gethsemane – we are told some of the places where Jesus made his 'retreat'. It would seem to be staggering arrogance on our part to believe that what the Son of God needed we do not – that somehow we can manage, whereas he, filled with the Spirit and called to do his Father's work (John 9.4), needed time to be quiet and pray.

It is that same need that more and more Christians are recognizing. It is quite distinct from the buzz we may get from attending a large Christian convention like Spring Harvest or Greenbelt. Those are occasions for inspiration and instruction, as well as fellowship with many like-minded Christians. A retreat, by contrast, is a withdrawal from company, apart from the company of God. There may be others sharing the place, and even being led by the same retreat conductor, but this is an occasion for silence, for minds focused solely on our own relationship with God. This may sound (and could be, if treated as an indulgence) very selfish, yet both the example and the teaching of Jesus provide a corrective.

As we have seen, Jesus withdrew to pray – indeed, after the death of John the Baptist he led his disciples away to a 'desert place' for a 'retreat' (Mark 6.30, 31) – an opportunity, one imagines, to reflect on what had happened, be open to the Father's will in the new situation and focus afresh on their spiritual priorities. In the Sermon on the Mount, he gave explicit instructions about the inner devotional life of the disciple. 'Whenever you pray', he said, 'do not be like the hypocrites; for they love to stand and pray in the synagogues and at the street corners, so that they may be seen by others. Truly I tell you, they have received their reward. But whenever you pray, go into your room and shut the door and pray to your Father who is in secret; and your Father who sees in secret will reward you' (Matthew 6.5–6).

There is obviously an important place in the Christian life for public worship, for corporate prayer, for the inspiration and support of true fellowship. Yet alongside these, as the example and teaching of Jesus shows, there is also a place for quiet, for solitude, for space to reflect and pray alone. To go on retreat is effectively to 'shut the door of your room' and in that 'secret' place unburden yourself to the One who always hears and is never far away from us.

When I conduct a retreat (or 'quiet day', as some like to call them), I always tell those taking part that it is *their* retreat. There is no 'programme', no agenda. Various things may be provided – talks, a Communion service, some reflective music in a side room. But each individual makes his or her own retreat. It is up to them to decide what would enhance that experience and what might detract from it. For some, who come on retreat burdened with mountains of cares – work, home, family, health – it is wonderfully healing just to be quiet, to have space, freedom, privacy. It's also true that the opportunity to speak privately and confidentially with the retreat conductor may provide an important way of release from a burden, care or personal failure which they have borne alone for too long. Sometimes, in contrast, we simply need to be alone with God. As the Bible makes clear over and over again, things can be learnt in the desert that can never be learnt in the town.

Much prayer bombards God with requests. The retreatant will more likely be in listening than demanding mode. 'This is my Son, my Beloved,' said the heavenly voice at the transfiguration of Jesus. 'Listen to him!' (Mark 9.7). Rather like an irritating radio interviewer who keeps interrupting his guests' questions, sometimes we talk so much that we hear nothing. A retreat is primarily a listening experience: 'Speak Lord, your servant is listening' (1 Samuel 3.9).

An essential element of listening is silence! Sometimes it may be that God's voice is drowned out by our own words. That's why silence is a normal and fundamental practice on retreat. I usually say that those taking part may speak to God as much as they like, and to the retreat conductor as much as they need, but not to each other! Sometimes the silence may be lifted for meals, to enable retreatants at least to greet each other, but it is the silence that many people remember about their first experience of a retreat.

Silence is not simply the absence of sound. It is much more positive and creative than that. When Elijah, in a fit of depression, was ready to throw in the towel in the face of the furious opposition of the queen, Jezebel, and her Baalite priests, he was drawn by the Lord to Mount Horeb. There, sheltering in a cave, he experienced various climatic traumas – a fierce gale, an earthquake and then what the Bible calls 'a fire' – perhaps thunderbolts. He doubtless wondered if God was speaking to him through these dramatic phenomena, but in fact when the divine message came it was in the 'sound of sheer silence'

(1 Kings 19.12). How then did he hear it? The answer surely must be that the inner ear of faith heard the message that would have been drowned out by the raging of the weather. 'Sheer silence' can speak to us, if the Lord is in the silence.

The experience of countless people down the Christian ages is that there is healing and renewal in silence. That is probably the primary blessing of a retreat. Yes, in the quiet we can speak to God. Yes, the retreat conductor may have words of wisdom for our ears. But it is the waiting heart that truly hears.

For reflection

For God alone my soul in silence waits.

Psalm 62.1

(Jesus) came out and went, as was his custom, to the Mount of Olives; and the disciples followed him. When he reached the place, he said to them, 'Pray that you may not come into the time of trial.' Then he withdrew from them about a stone's throw, knelt down, and prayed, 'Father, if you are willing, remove this cup from me; yet, not my will but yours be done.' Then an angel from heaven appeared to him and gave him strength.

Luke 22.39–42

Breathe through the heats of our desire
thy coolness and thy balm;
let sense be dumb, let flesh retire;
speak through the earthquake, wind and fire,
O still small voice of calm.

John Greenleaf Whittier

17

TRAVELLING WITH PURPOSE

Going on pilgrimage

I've never really liked rambling. It has always seemed to me a rather pointless exercise – walking for the sake of walking. Being inclined to idleness, I'd rather sit and talk, though if there's a destination to be reached I can enjoy walking in company. Not everyone agrees with me, of course – the Easter 'parish ramble' used to be a big event in the life of our north London church. All the same, I was pleased to be assured by a preacher long ago that the Christian life was not a ramble (a journey without a destination). Rather it was a pilgrimage: going somewhere with purpose.

The Christian life as pilgrimage is a common enough biblical metaphor, even though the actual word is not used, because a pilgrim is on a journey of faith. The first Christians were called 'followers of the Way', echoing the words of Jesus about his being the 'way' to the Father (John 14.6). St Paul said that he had not yet 'arrived' on that journey, but he pressed on towards the goal (Philippians 3.12). Bunyan's classic story of *The Pilgrim's Progress* charts the journey of Christian through many hazards – the Slough of Despond, the Giant Despair, Vanity Fair – on his way to the Celestial City. At baptism, we often pray for the candidate as he or she joins the 'pilgrim people of God' – fellow-travellers on a journey.

In fact, a genuine pilgrimage is a microcosm of the Christian life. It begins with an act of faith and commitment. It progresses through many challenges, tribulations, trials and joys as the journey of faith continues. Eventually it arrives at its destination, the place of blessing, the gates of heaven itself. Perhaps that concept lies behind the feeling that a pilgrimage ought to be difficult! As Jesus said, 'Those who endure to the end will be saved' (Mark 13.13). Part of the journey of the pilgrim necessarily involves overcoming set-backs and disappointments. Not only that, but we instinctively feel that it should not be *too* comfortable – I've never been happy with the notion of a 'pilgrimage' in an air-conditioned coach!

On the other hand, the pilgrim will also experience many positive things. There will be, very often, the encouragement of one's companions on the journey, the food provided for the traveller – the *viaticum*, the places of rest and refreshment on the way, and above all the constant presence of a Guide who has said 'I am with you all the ways' (literally) (Matthew 28.20).

So the idea of the Christian life as a journey, with a starting point of faith and baptism and the kingdom of heaven as our final destination, is well known. As a result, our everyday experiences of travel become metaphors of our spiritual progress. Sometimes the journey seems smooth, the 'connections' reassuring, the company warm and supportive. At other times we hit setbacks and obstacles. Far from making progress, we seem to be slipping backwards. Suddenly, we are no longer surrounded by encouraging friends – the journey seems lonely and unrewarding. All of this becomes the language of pilgrimage, as Christians have always understood it. We can, if we wish, describe a holiday in the Holy Land, staying in excellent hotels and travelling in comfort, as a 'pilgrimage' (and I have), but the true pilgrim expects the journey to be challenging, demanding, even sacrificial. To arrive at the destination tired but full of joy at reaching the end of the journey is to experience the pilgrim's reward.

Pilgrimages began early in church history, as believers made their way to places associated with the earthly life of Jesus. Helen, the mother of the Emperor Constantine, went to the Holy Land in 326CE, visiting many places associated with the ministry of Jesus and having basilicas built to mark the sites. Among them were the Mount of Olives and the presumed place of the birth of Jesus in Bethlehem, as well as the site of the crucifixion – again marked by the building of a church. These became places of pilgrimage for Christians, though the later invasions by the Saracens sometimes made them inaccessible.

There is a tradition, for which there is some evidence, that the empty tomb of Jesus was also a place of pilgrimage for Christians in the very early years of the Church. Some scholars even argue that Mark's Gospel was written as a 'text-book' for those visiting the site. Whether that was so or not, the idea of making a pilgrimage to a sacred site was soon established, with Christians travelling vast distances to pray not only at places associated with the biblical story but also at the tombs and memorials of saints and martyrs. By the time of Chaucer and his *Canterbury Tales* pilgrimages were big business, with people travelling in groups across Europe – from Britain, for instance, to Rome or Spain – and across the British Isles to Lindisfarne, St David's or (after the murder of Thomas a Becket) Canterbury.

This travelling was not done in luxury, by any means, and certainly many did it as a genuine act of religious devotion, but the pilgrims expected hospitality from people in the villages and towns through which they passed. They wore a scallop shell badge, and this would generally guarantee them a warm welcome and a meal on the way. The better off pilgrims tended to stay in inns on the journey, and – like Chaucer's pilgrims – regarded it all as a pleasant pastime rather than a rigorous spiritual discipline. Sadly, in the manner of the time and consistently with the principle of original sin, it wasn't long before unscrupulous people produced bogus relics and invented stories to endow places with miraculous properties or hitherto unknown connections with various saints. From this the unpleasant business of the sale of Indulgences – papal pardons provided for naïve pilgrims in return for a cash contribution – lined the coffers of the Church, and often the pockets of the 'Pardoners' as well.

Chaucer's book provides an undoubtedly fair picture both of the good and the bad elements of pilgrimage in his time – the genuinely devout, seeking 'the holy blissful martyr' in order to solicit his prayers, and the unscrupulous exploiters of the gullible and ignorant, more interested in earthly returns than heavenly reward.

Since the Middle Ages the nature of pilgrimage has tended to change. People usually make a pilgrimage for a specific purpose, which includes prayer and worship at the chosen site as well as reflection on its significance in the story of the faith. The great pilgrim sites are often associated, of course, with the incarnation: the Church of the Nativity in Bethlehem, the sea of Galilee and the village of Capernaum, the Church of the Holy Sepulchre in Jerusalem, and the Via Dolorosa. However, all over the world there are places of Christian pilgrimage. Lourdes is probably the best known, but Santiago de Compostela, Medugorje, Walsingham in England, Assisi, and of course Rome are also major sites of pilgrimage. It doesn't really seem to matter if the historic credentials of the site have been questioned or even disproved. The blessing, the pilgrim says, is in the atmosphere of prayer and faith which such places seem to accumulate. In modern times the journey is not usually very demanding, though many pilgrims to Santiago, for instance, opt to walk enormous distances across Spain to get there, and undoubtedly get closer to the heart of true pilgrimage by doing so.

The vital element of a pilgrimage is not in fact the destination but the journey, though arriving at the desired haven crowns the endeavour. Most pilgrims travel in company, and that fellowship of purpose adds an element of shared prayer and mutual witness which can transform the whole experience. That has been my own experience in the Holy Land, in Assisi and in Rome.

Those who wish to try the experience of a pilgrimage do not have to cross the world to do so. In the British Isles there are places which evoke just that spirit of prayer and holiness, and a thoughtful journey to them will seldom be wasted. Iona, with its splendid abbey on a wave-tossed island, is certainly one, Canterbury is undoubtedly another. St David's, on the west coast of Wales, takes us back, as Iona does, to the great days of the Celtic Church and her missionaries. The abbey at Dorchester on Thames is a neglected jewel for the pilgrim – near the place in the river Thames where Birinus baptized a pagan king of the Saxons and by that act drew a whole tribe of people to Christ. Armagh in Ireland, York, the lonely cell of Julian of Norwich, and the places associated with countless local saints and martyrs – the list is endless. Every country in Christendom has its holy sites, and many of them are places of pilgrimage. In essence, all any pilgrim needs is the intention, the unhurried time to journey and the grace to turn both the travelling and the arriving into an enriching spiritual experience.

For reflection

Who would true valour see,
Let him come hither;

One here will constant be,
come wind, come weather;
There's no discouragement
Shall make him once relent
His first avowed intent
To be a pilgrim.

John Bunyan

This one thing I do: forgetting what lies behind and straining forward to what lies ahead, I press on toward the goal for the prize of the heavenly call of God in Christ Jesus.

Philippians 3.13, 14

May God, who has received you by baptism into his Church, pour upon you the riches of his grace, that within the company of Christ's pilgrim people you may daily be renewed by his anointing Spirit, and come to the inheritance of the saints in glory.

Common Worship, Baptism service

18

RULE OF LIFE

Daily discipline

There is a built-in paradox in the Christian life, one which any reader of the letters of St Paul, for instance, will recognize. On the one hand, we have his stern warnings to the Christians at Galatia not to submit to man-made rules and regulations. 'How can you want to be enslaved to them again?' he asks. 'You are observing special days, and months and seasons, and years. I am afraid that my work for you may have been wasted' (4.9–11). On the other hand, as we have seen, we have the apostle himself determined to go to Jerusalem for the Passover – observing a season? – and he is not averse to giving very precise instructions, 'directions' even, about their financial giving to the work of the church (1 Corinthians 16.1–4).

In fact, he is writing about two different things, an 'enslavement' to a system (what he calls 'the law', though he is absolutely clear that he is not talking about the God-given moral law, which has permanent authority) on the one hand, and the freedom the believer has voluntarily and willingly to live a disciplined life on the other. The freedom we have in Christ is not, as he explains to the Galatians, 'an opportunity for self-indulgence' (5.11), nor does it preclude the need to shape our lives according to the demands of the gospel.

So it's not surprising that from early times in the Church Christians have subscribed to various 'rules of life'. Such rules were, of course, an essential element of the life of religious communities, the most famous of which is certainly the Rule of Benedict, dating back to the sixth century. This came to be recognized as the basis of almost every other monastic rule right through the Middle Ages, and has influenced many ordinary Christians in shaping a 'rule of life' for themselves.

Benedict's Rule included, as we should expect, the reading of Scripture, especially the Psalms, together with periods of prayer and worship throughout the day – the 'Offices'. It included provision for manual work, for rest and for meals. It outlined an appropriate Christian lifestyle – modesty, frugality, a disciplined thought life, generosity and care. Some of Benedict's Rule could only be appropriate in a monastic setting, but the pattern of prayer, Scripture, reflection and lifestyle became the model for many Christians in their daily lives. Today the Third Order Franciscans – lay people who accept a rule of life following Franciscan principles but adapted to living in a secular setting – follow much the same model. An important element of that Rule, as we might expect, is a 'modest lifestyle'. It would be inconsistent of a Third Order Franciscan to drive a gas-guzzling motor car!

The question of whether or not to adopt a 'rule of life' must be a matter of free choice if it is not to be what St Paul once stigmatized as 'will-worship'. But such a rule, freely entered into, need not be a legalistic burden, more a kind of bench-mark of what we regard as the standard of discipline which we desire to set for ourselves.

Once we have decided to adopt a 'rule of life', we are faced with the task of shaping it. There are a number of existing 'rules', including the Franciscan one to which I have referred, but it is probably wise to be realistic about the constraints of time, family, travel and work before creating a rule which simply leads to our constantly feeling guilty of failure. Taking the basic elements of the disciplined Christian life, we can see that prayer, Bible reading, reflection and quiet are required ingredients. We then need to determine when and how often during the day we can practically engage in them. In addition to those 'private' elements of a rule of life, there are the corporate ones – joining in worship and prayer with our fellow-Christians, gathering at the Lord's Table regularly to receive holy communion, engaging in Christian service of others and bearing a witness to friends, neighbours and colleagues. Alongside these it would seem appropriate to incorporate issues of discipline in daily life – how we spend our money, what we do with and how we regard our possessions, our use of leisure and an avoidance of ostentatious displays of wealth. All of these can become elements of a rule of life.

It may reasonably be argued that Christians should be doing all these things without the need of a 'rule', but the harsh truth is that most of us find in everyday life that without regular disciplines we simply end up in disarray. So we have regular disciplines for all sorts of ordinary things – cleaning our teeth, changing the bed-clothes, doing the shopping, paying the bills, even mowing the lawn. There is a security in method which is very familiar in the pattern of our daily lives – what time we leave the house in the morning for work, where we buy our newspaper, how we hang up our clothes at night. We don't see this as 'legalism', but simply as a way of living a 'normal' life.

In much the same way, to have some shape and method to our Christian discipleship need not lead us into legalism but in fact can liberate us to live a fulfilling and balanced spiritual life. To know when we usually pray, how we go about it, what Scripture we are currently reading, when we join with our fellow-Christians in worship and service, is to enjoy true freedom.

In much the same way, the discipline of learning to play the piano frees the pianist to enjoy to the full the experience of making music. Without the discipline, the result is nothing more than a cacophony. It is all very well to speak of spontaneity in music making, as some people do, but it is best if spontaneity is linked with competence. What a rule of life gives to the Christian is a competency in discipleship within which it is possible to exercise enormous spontaneity, joy and freedom.

On the building of a Christian rule of life the following questions probably need to be addressed:

- When and where shall I pray? How often?
- Shall I follow an existing form of prayer and praise?
- How shall I approach on a regular basis the reading of Scripture, including the Psalms?
- Do I need to specify when and how often I receive communion?
- Do I need to specify when and how often I share in worship and prayer with my fellow-Christians?
- What acts of loving service of others shall I engage in? How, and when?
- What should be the principles of a Christian lifestyle for me?
- How shall I, as a Christian, serve the wider community?

We may feel that one way to answer a number of these questions would be to adopt an existing Office for our prayers and Scripture reading, or use a Bible reading routine such as those provided by the Bible Reading Fellowship, Scripture Union and the International Bible Reading Association. We might turn to the Third Order Franciscan Rule for suggestions about Christian lifestyle. The questions about service and witness might be ones to discuss with other members of our church, or with our priest or pastor.

In a sense, how we go about establishing a rule of life is a private and voluntary matter. We may well wish to discuss it with a pastor or spiritual director. We shall certainly make it a matter of prayer. What is certain, surely, is that for every Christian there is a way to live the life of Christ, and though this may vary from person to person, the need to be clear in our minds what it is for us is absolute.

For reflection

When Jesus came to Nazareth, where he had been brought up, he went to the synagogue on the sabbath day, as was his custom.

Luke 4.16

The end of all things is at hand; therefore be serious and discipline yourselves for the sake of your prayers.

1 Peter 4.7

Now, discipline always seems painful rather than pleasant at the time, but later it yields the peaceful fruit of righteousness to those who have been trained by it. Therefore lift your drooping hands and strengthen your weak knees, and make straight paths for your feet, so that what is lame may not be put out of joint, but rather be healed. Pursue peace with everyone, and the holiness without which no one will see the Lord.

Hebrews 12.11–13

We must be anchored in self-discipline if we are to venture successfully in freedom.

Harold E. Kohn

19

SPIRITUAL DIRECTION

The 'helper alongside'

I suppose a 'Spiritual Director' might sound to some people like the executive producer of a ghost movie or the boss of a chain of wine shops. In fact, it's a title with which more and more Christians are becoming familiar. A spiritual director is not your confessor (the priest to whom people can confess their sins) nor is he or she your counsellor, offering a listening ear to your problems and anxieties and, in due course, perhaps suggesting appropriate courses of action to deal with them. A spiritual director is a person who helps you to plan and then work out in practice a disciplined, authentic and balanced Christian life, of the kind we considered in the last chapter.

The spiritual director *par excellence* is of course the Holy Spirit, given to the individual Christian and to the Church to be a source of constant prompting, directing and support. In John's Gospel the Spirit is referred to as the advocate, or in some translations comforter, helper or counsellor. All of these are attempts to translate the Greek word *parakletos*, sometimes anglicized as 'paraclete'. Literally this title means something like 'alongside-helper' (think of our words 'paramedic' or 'parachute'). The Holy Spirit is given to us as a helper, but of a particular kind. He (or she – the word is feminine in Hebrew) is 'on our side' (hence the term 'advocate'), he pleads our cause. But he is also the voice of conscience, rebuking and correcting when necessary, and a guide in matters of faith and practice. He 'leads us into the truth' (John 16.13); he not only helps us to pray but sometimes prays through us (Romans 8.26–27). He sets our goals and he guides our steps.

Of course, no one would suggest that any human spiritual director could equal the range of gifts and wisdom available to the Holy Spirit of God. No human friend or guide can replace for us that essential presence of the Holy Spirit in the life of the believer and the Church. However, the role of a spiritual director is to try to help me to hear the Spirit's voice and respond to his promptings. He or she will sometimes act as the voice of conscience: why have you abandoned night prayers? What has gone wrong with your relationship with the local church? Sometimes the Director will simply listen; sometimes spend time praying with us, and sometimes probe gently but insistently at the areas of our spiritual life that are exhibiting weakness or even failure.

The wise spiritual director does not seek to act as an infallible source of wisdom – far from it. This particular 'helper alongside' is not there to give advice, but to help us to find the answer for ourselves. Sometimes a large part of a session will be occupied by silence; always it will be saturated with prayer. With our director we can be frank and open – indeed, there is no point in having one if we are going to play games of spiritual hide-and-seek. We have agreed a balanced and authentic pattern of daily living. The director stands by us not as an enforcer but as a sympathetic but honest friend.

Many Christians nowadays have found it an enormous help to have a spiritual director. This may simply be someone they know and respect as a wise and godly Christian – someone they trust (because the role requires a high degree of confidentiality) and someone whose insights and prayers they value. So far as I know there is no formal qualification for spiritual directors; you can't get a diploma in it! Yet most of us can recognize the sort of person who could fulfill that role for us, though it is a decision we may wish to share with others, such as our priest or pastor.

If we approach someone to enquire whether they would be prepared to take on the role for us, an initial meeting may help to determine whether this would be right or not. Both 'sides' must be free to say 'no', without any feeling that this is in some way a judgment on the other person. It isn't. It is simply a recognition that for some reason – often too elusive to articulate – this arrangement might not work well. Neither party should feel rejected.

However, when both parties feel happy with the proposal, it is usual for some kind of working agreement to be drawn up. How often and when will you meet, and for how long? What are the particular areas of concern that the disciple would wish the director to address? Will there be some arrangement by which the spiritual director can be contacted at moments of particular concern or need? On the director's side, there may be questions of accountability, of confidentiality and of time. If travel is involved, it is only right that the question of expenses should be addressed. It is better if these are dealt with at the start, rather than left to emerge, possibly at inconvenient occasions.

To have someone with whom one can speak frankly and freely about one's spiritual journey is remarkably liberating. All too often we simply bottle up our anxieties, or engage in desperate but fruitless self-condemnation. There are, truth to tell, few 'new' problems in the area of discipleship. The likelihood is that someone, somewhere, has walked this way before us, encountered these difficulties, and experienced these set-backs. A wise spiritual director will recognize that fact, and can often draw on his or her own experience, or that of others, to reassure and guide the perplexed soul.

It's hard to find a precise equivalent of a spiritual director in the New Testament, probably because by the nature of the role it is a private and confidential one. However, anyone reading the last chapter of the book of Romans will be irresistibly drawn to the idea that among all these wonderful supportive fellow-Christians named there were several who performed this ministry – perhaps even for Paul himself. Phoebe had been his 'benefactor', an ambiguous term which could well include spiritual support and guidance. Andronicus and Junia were in prison with the apostle – surely they supported each other during that terrible experience? Persis is 'beloved', Rufus is 'chosen' – and his mother had been a 'mother' to Paul. All or any of these may have fulfilled at least part of the role of a spiritual director for him, or for others in the church at Rome. In any case, the need creates the call, and the call discovers the person who responds to it. Every Christian needs help and support on the often lonely journey of faith. Finding the right companion on the way is what choosing a spiritual director is all about.

For reflection

Teach and admonish one another in all wisdom.

Colossians 3.16

And we have confidence in the Lord concerning you, that you are doing and will go on doing the things that we command. May the Lord direct your hearts to the love of God and to the steadfastness of Christ.

2 Thessalonians 3.4–5

The impulse of love that leads us to the doorway of a friend is the voice of God within and we need not be afraid to follow it.

Agnes Sanford

No one can develop freely in this world and live a full life without feeling understood by at least one person.

Paul Tournier

20

THE SACRED SIGNS

The 'lesser' sacraments

The word 'sacrament' entered Christian vocabulary in early days. It's the Latin equivalent of the Greek word for 'mystery', and was used to describe the means by which Christians shared in the mystery revealed in Jesus. So it was applied to baptism and the meal of the Eucharist. For the first thousand years of Christian history, however, it also had a wider meaning. St Augustine defined a sacrament as 'a visible form of invisible grace', and applied it much more widely – for instance, to Scripture, the Creed and the Lord's Prayer. Anything which had an outward form which revealed in some way a spiritual truth was, in this thinking, sacramental.

From about the time of the Great Schism, when the Western Church split from the Eastern Church, the meaning was narrowed. To be 'valid' a sacrament must have been instituted by Jesus Christ. Clearly baptism and the Lord's Supper passed that test, but the Church also recognized five other sacraments: confirmation, penance, extreme unction, 'orders' and marriage. There is no clear evidence that several of these were 'instituted by Christ' in the literal sense; the connection was regarded as implicit. At the Reformation what are generally known as the 'lesser sacraments' were separated from the 'dominical' ones (those clearly instituted by the Lord), and in practice most churches in the reformed traditions have regarded the others as, in some cases, states of life approved by God (marriage), devout practices (penance, anointing with oil) or extensions of the fundamental sacraments (confirmation). 'Orders' clearly have sacramental qualities as 'visible forms of invisible grace' and it might be assumed that Jesus 'instituted' them when he set aside his apostles and commissioned them to carry his message into all the world, but there has been disagreement about regarding ordination to an office in the Church as a sacrament.

This whole discussion can be clouded by arguments over definitions, but what is clear is that there are certain signs and symbols which the Holy Spirit has used all through the history of the Church as means of grace – and that these signs are wider than the two universally recognized 'sacraments' of baptism and the Lord's Supper.

In fact, much if not most of the day-to-day experience of the Christian, and of the life of the Church, is 'sacramental'. That's to say, it is a combination of outward 'signs' and inward 'graces'. That would be true of Bible reading (we have to pick it up and read it before we can be open to its work in our lives) gratitude (we feel grateful, but generally need to express that in words or actions for it to make a difference). As we have seen already with anointing, or the use of icons in prayer, the outward sign is not magical – but when it is allied to an inward desire or motion of the will, then it becomes a means of grace.

Of the usual list of 'lesser sacraments' the one that makes this point most powerfully is penance. This is a concept largely foreign to Protestant or Reformed Christianity, because it appears to suggest that we can bring something – some deed, or work, or sacrifice – to our own forgiveness, thus diminishing the completeness of what Christ has done for us. Obviously that danger is an ever present one: we do not 'earn' forgiveness, it is a gift of

God in response to the sacrifice of his Son. That is classical Christian doctrine. We bring nothing to our salvation except the sin from which we seek to be redeemed, and the faith that through Jesus Christ that sin can be forgiven.

However, human nature being what it is, our words of repentance often leave us feeling unsure. Did I really, truly and completely express repentance for that particular sin? Were my words genuine? How can I persuade myself that I have 'truly and earnestly' repented (as the old Prayer Book puts it)? In biblical times people signified their repentance by putting dust and ashes on their heads and wearing sackcloth – outward signs to those around that they were aware of their sins and had repented them. There are many examples in the Old Testament, such as Esther 4.1, Job 42.6, Jeremiah 6.26, and many, many more. It's true that Jesus told his disciples not to use such external signs of repentance, because they had been abused by people who wished to make a public display of their piety, making sure everyone knew that they had atoned for their sins by fasting and disfiguring themselves. The disciples of Jesus were to fast, but to do so privately, without display. We may assume that if a truly penitent person had marked their repentance with sackcloth and ashes in private, it would not have earned this rebuke.

Of course, Christian penance has seldom involved sackcloth and ashes, at any rate in the literal sense. What it has done, and continues to do for many Christians in the Catholic tradition, is to provide an outward mark of their inner repentance. They wonder, Did I truly repent? Were my words adequate to express my shame and sorrow? But they can recall not just what they said, but what they *did*. And while they may question their words, and even their feelings, they can't question the memory of an action. Of course the action does not earn forgiveness.

That's not what it represents. What it can do is remind us of the reality of our repentance. As the poet John Donne prayed, 'Teach me how to repent, for that's as good/ As if thou hadst sealed my pardon with thy blood'. Many of us long to know that our repentance is real. The action serves to remind us that it is and that it was painful and costly for us – though not as painful and costly as it was for Jesus to pay the price of our forgiveness.

Traditionally acts of penance, usually proposed by the priest at confession, involved the recitation of prayers (ten 'Hail Mary's, for instance). In recent times those acts of penance have often been more closely related to the nature of the sin being confessed. Reparation, an apology, or a piece of neighbourly service may help to remind the penitent that repentance does involve cost – initially the swallowing of our pride and the unconditional recognition that we were wrong and God was right. Repentance isn't easy. As Martin Luther said, 'The truest repentance is to do it no more' – and that involves a discipline of will and self-discipline. There is no such thing as 'cheap grace', in the words of Dietrich Bonhoeffer, mostly because grace cost Jesus everything, but also because, while we cannot 'earn' grace, which is a free gift, it is the truly penitent heart that receives forgiveness.

Marriage offers a similar example of sacramental grace. The couple may have every intention of living faithfully and lovingly together, but it is the public utterance of their vows which is the outward sign of marriage. No amount of inner intention or shared affection can effect it without those words, spoken before witnesses. Both the inner will and the external sign are required before a relationship can be described as marriage. Of course it is the inner intention that is fundamental: without it, marriage is a sham. But without the external confession, it is a purely private arrangement, and the grace that is associated with matrimony flows from the whole sacramental process.

Once this process is accepted and understood, one can begin to see how it undergirds so much of Christian spirituality. We are physical beings as well as spiritual entities. Our words and actions are the outward signs of what and who we are. It is true, of course, that God reads our hearts, but sometimes our heart's deepest conviction needs to be expressed to become part of who we are. St Paul makes precisely this point in his Letter to the church at Rome. 'If you confess with your lips that Jesus is Lord and believe in your heart that God raised him from the dead, you will be saved. For one believes with the heart and so is justified, and one confesses with the mouth and so is saved' (10.9–10). There it is: the inward belief, the outward confession, the two parts of a sacrament combining to confirm salvation. Right at the heart of Christian faith, at its very beginning, there is the sacrament of the spiritual and the physical, the intention and the action. There is nothing 'lesser' about that!

For reflection

We look not at what can be seen but at what cannot be seen; for what can be seen is temporary, but what cannot be seen is eternal.

2 Corinthians 4.18

When Jesus had been baptized, just as he came up from the water, suddenly the heavens were opened to him and he saw the Spirit of God descending like a dove and alighting on him. And a voice from heaven said, 'This is my Son, the Beloved, with whom I am well pleased.'

Matthew 3.16–17

God did extraordinary miracles through Paul, so that when the handkerchiefs or aprons that had touched his skin were brought to the sick, their diseases left them, and the evil spirits came out of them.

Acts 19.12

For this reason I remind you to rekindle the gift of God that is within you through the laying on of my hands; for God did not give us a spirit of cowardice, but rather a spirit of power and of love and of self-discipline.

2 Timothy 1.6–7

21

IGNATIAN SPIRITUALITY

The consecrated life

The story of the life of Ignatius of Loyola is an indelible part of the history of the Roman Catholic Church, and of the Reformation period in church history. A one-time soldier, after his conversion he carried something of the organization and discipline of the military life into his spirituality, so that the religious Order which he eventually founded, the Society of Jesus, or the Jesuits, as they are universally known, became in effect the Pope's 'army'. Largely in response to the Lutheran and Calvinist movements, they were the spearhead of a papal counter-attack. Their chief weapons were education and preaching, but they also recognized that the medieval Catholic Church had many serious weaknesses and failings. Many of these were addressed in what became known as the 'Counter-Reformation', but it was probably the Jesuits, over the next century, who did most to show that the Catholic Church still had vitality, a robust faith and a sense of mission.

The Jesuits vowed absolute obedience to the Roman pontiff, and followed a rigorous spiritual discipline of prayer, sacrament and study. The 'Spiritual Exercises' of Ignatius became required study for all Roman Catholic ordinands (and still are, very widely), as well as a source of inspiration to many Christians in other traditions. As the Reformed scholar J. I. Packer has written, 'They remain a potent aid to self-knowledge and devotion to the Lord Jesus, even for those outside the Catholicism in which they are so strongly rooted'.

The exercises form a four-fold programme of meditation and instruction. The first part reflects on sin and its effects and consequences. The second considers the role of Jesus as Lord and King. The third is a devotional reflection on his cross and passion, and the fourth on his risen life.

In this way they reflect a truly rounded experience of the Christian life. The first section requires disciples to examine themselves, and offers various tools towards accomplishing this. A chief mark of the Exercises is their ability to help the Christian to see his or her life in the light of the life of Christ, and to judge themselves by that standard alone. The seriousness of sin, and the consequences of its taking root in the soul, are forcefully set out. There is no danger of the person following the Exercises being in any doubt about the dire consequence of unrepented sin, or of any compromise with moral failure.

The second section offers a contrasting picture, reflecting on the Lordship of Christ. Those who claim him as Saviour are duty bound also to recognize him as their Lord, Master and King. In this way Ignatius lifts the believer's eyes above the negative images of sin and failure to contemplate the victorious Lord of life, the source of forgiveness and salvation.

The third section focuses specifically on the passion of Christ. Like many mystical writers of the period, Ignatius dwells on the physical nature of the suffering of Christ, but always with the intention of drawing the disciple into a more intense devotion to the crucified Saviour. This was very much a part of his own experience of inner conversion, and he is able to combine the language of medieval devotion, which invited the believer to be drawn into the heart of the crucified, with a challenge to live what St Paul called the crucified life in daily discipline.

The last section is an exposition of the risen life – not only the risen life of Christ, now exalted to the right hand of the majesty on high, but the life of the disciple lived in the light of the resurrection. We are called to share the risen life of Christ. Again in the language of St Paul, 'I have been crucified with Christ; and it is no longer I who live, but it is Christ who lives in me. And the life I now live in the flesh I live by faith in the Son of God, who loved me and gave himself for me' (Galatians 2.19–20).

The part of Ignatian spirituality best known today is probably his particular approach to the reading of Scripture. Many retreat conductors employ or recommend this approach, which is well suited to a situation in which the reader has time, quiet and space to approach a Bible story in an imaginative rather than analytical or educational way. The reader (or listener, if this story or incident is being read or narrated) is invited to place themselves *inside* the narrative, not as a spectator or observer, but as a participant. So, in the passion scene, for instance, one might take on the position of a soldier in the execution squad, or one of the condemned thieves, or Mary or John – or, indeed, a sceptical onlooker.

From this position, it may be possible to enter more deeply into the emotion and impact of the occasion, to share, to some extent, the feelings of a participant, to reflect how we might from our own perspective of faith or experience of life respond had we been there. The experience can be a very powerful one for some people. I have known some who have been moved to tears by it, though it has to be said that not all find it helpful and a few actually find it either too disturbing or too artificial. However, as a way of getting into the biblical narrative it is certainly worth considering, especially in the context of a retreat.

The Spiritual Exercises of Ignatius provide a structured programme of what might be called 'imaginative prayer' along these lines which takes, in its full form, about a month to complete. However, parts of it are frequently used on much shorter retreats, and some exercises, like the one on the Bible, can be adapted to a single day. What is essential, in the thought of Ignatius, is the will to exercise discipline, to create time and space for unhurried exploration and unencumbered listening. The object of the exercises is nothing less than the fully consecrated life – a life centred around Jesus Christ himself. His Order is unique in bearing simply the name of the Son of God – the 'Society of Jesus'. It is the cultivation of that 'society' for which he strove, and for which he urged his brothers to strive.

Ignatius believed that only in the presence of God can we fully understand ourselves. Consequently, he saw the life of prayer and meditation as the path to self-knowledge. In the light of that understanding Christians can engage with their perceived failings and short-comings, and recognize also their vocation and gifts. This is in some ways the opposite of self-analysis, because it is as we spend time in the company of Jesus that we understand ourselves, or rather our inner self is revealed to us.

In terms of Ignatian Spirituality this self-knowledge, and a complete and realistic consecration of life to Christ, are the fruit of an obedient will. His insistence on absolute obedience to Christ and the Church was for him a matter of willing submission to the authority of God. However, he recognized that this submission is not easily attained, because it runs counter to our fallen nature. Three vital elements in that submission or consecration of life were for him the understanding, the imagination and conscience.

Understanding is not to be seen as the acquisition of information but rather as openness to revelation. Through the Spiritual Exercises, he taught, the mind becomes open to the Word of God. The human mind – so rebellious and wilful – is exposed to the mind of the Creator and his wisdom.

Imagination is a cherished element in Ignatian spirituality. This is not an undisciplined or fanciful indulgence, but the God-given ability to 'imagine' in the sense of visualizing or opening the mind to images, words and sensations that are sacred. His own conversion came about through a mystical revelation in the monastery at Manresa, and though he was careful not to specify the precise ways in which each disciple would come to the point of consecration there is undoubtedly always a mystical element in his understanding of the believer's relationship with Christ. In some ways this stood in contrast to the more doctrinal and word-based approach of Reformers like Calvin and Knox, though of course there was always a mystical strand in Protestantism as well. Ignatius himself presents a paradox, for his fierce orthodoxy, in terms of obedience to the Church's teaching, was balanced by an intense inner life of what he called 'imaginative prayer'.

Conscience was the sentry at the gate of all of this. To act against conscience was sin, but the conscience must be informed by a true faith, by genuine understanding. Illuminated by the Holy Spirit, conscience would light our path and ensure that our imagination did not lead us astray.

As one can see, the Ignatian way is a powerful path of discipleship, demanding but rewarding, based on the principle of obedience but touched with the light of understanding and imagination. Though some have found it too rigorous and even authoritarian, many have been liberated by his vision of the life utterly and entirely consecrated to Jesus. All, surely, can learn something from a path so many have trodden, and with such rich reward.

For reflection

Prayers of St Ignatius of Loyola

Teach me, good Lord,
how to serve you as you deserve;
to give, and not to count the cost;
to fight, and not to mind the wounds;
to work, and not to long for rest;
to labour, and not to do it for any reward
less than knowing that I am doing your will,
through Jesus Christ our Lord.
Amen

Grant, O Lord, that my heart may neither desire nor seek anything but what is necessary for the fulfilment of Thy holy Will. May health or sickness, riches or poverty, honours or contempt, humiliations, leave my soul in that state of perfect detachment to which I desire to attain for Thy greater honour and Thy greater glory.
Amen

(Jesus prayed) I am not asking on behalf of the world, but on behalf of those whom you gave me, because they are yours ... But now I am coming to you, and I speak these things in the world so that they may have my joy made complete in themselves ... Sanctify them in the truth; your word is truth. As you have sent me into the world, so I have sent them into the world. And for their sakes I sanctify myself, so that they also may be sanctified in truth.

John 17.9, 13, 17–19

Let us work as if success depended upon ourselves alone; but with the heartfelt conviction that we are doing nothing and God everything.

St Ignatius Loyola

22

THE ROAD WELL
TRAVELLED

A new way of following old paths

We have been looking at what we might call the 'old paths' of spirituality – paths largely ignored at the present time by many Christians. As we have done so, we have been exploring various ways of 'being Christian' which have been valuable to countless disciples down the centuries. But it isn't enough simply to say 'return to the old paths'. After all, as the old Latin tag says, 'Times change, and we change with them'. It is probably unhelpful to argue that simply adopting, in a slavish way, the spiritual disciplines of an earlier age will automatically make us better Christians now. What we need, as the title of this chapter suggests, is a 'new way' of following the old paths.

We live in an age of questions rather than answers, but many of them are very fundamental questions, and simply to ask them is in fact to begin a spiritual journey. 'Is there a God?' 'Does the universe have meaning and purpose?' 'In the vastness of the cosmos, how can I, as an individual, find value and significance?' 'Why, when so much about human beings is explained by scientific analysis, do I feel as though I am much more than a collection of physical particles attached to an onboard computer?'

'To find God, must I subscribe to a set of propositions that I find incredible?' And perhaps most basically – to quote Stephen Hawking – 'Why does the universe bother to exist?'

All these are ultimately questions about meaning, but they are also intensely personal – and many of them are exclusively 'modern', products of a society where belief in a divinity is not universal. However, recent research has suggested that human babies are, as it were, 'wired' from birth to believe in God. It is our default position as human beings. We do not have to learn belief, but we do have to learn unbelief. It's strange to read this scientific support for the kind of ideas Wordsworth expressed two hundred years ago in his 'Ode on Intimations of Immortality'. The child, in his thought, came from heaven 'trailing clouds of glory'. It was only with the passing of time that 'shades of the prison house' closed in around the growing boy.

Perhaps, then, we are made for belief. In defiance of the evidence of our own eyes that dead things remain dead, our race has constantly held to the conviction that there is more to life than a brief spell on the surface of this impermanent planet. With astonishing courage, we have looked into the universe unblinking, and in an odd way felt that its Creator is loving and not malign. We feel at home in what Christians may call 'the Father's world'.

Of course human beings have always thought such thoughts, but the modern world sets them in an altogether more challenging context. If we are to explore the old paths in search of spiritual nurture, then we will have to explore them as citizens of the world of the twenty-first century, not the fifth or the fifteenth. There is, I am convinced, rich treasure here, but we shall have to mine it for ourselves, often with different tools, though with the same spiritual longing as our forebears. When Augustine of Hippo famously said that God has made us for himself, 'and we are restless till we find ourselves in him', he was talking our language. We understand and feel what he meant. But few of us would find the spiritual disciplines of the fourth century helpful in the way that he did. The beliefs which we hold with our Christian forebears are the same – we hold the 'apostolic faith'. But the context in which we live, the daily agenda of our lives, is so different that we need to find new ways of living spiritually. Much that they valued will be valuable to us, as we have seen, but even that which is of permanent worth, rather than simply culturally timely, will need to be worked out in the context of twenty-first-century living. The important thing is not the mechanics, but the meaning; not finding the right method, but the true experience of God.

David Tracy has said in his book *The Spirituality Revolution* that we are 'caught in a difficult moment in history, stuck between a secular system we have outgrown and a religious system we cannot fully embrace'. Perhaps Thomas Aquinas, from centuries earlier, offers a way of escape from the modern dilemma: 'In order to move beyond our present limits, we have to allow the possibility that it is our own vision that is deficient, that it is we who are lacking'. It requires some courage to be willing to explore a new way of walking an old path, and perhaps for some Christians it may involve an element of risk. But the potential rewards could be life-changing.

Few people today would have many misgivings about the emphasis of Ignatius on imagination, but many – possibly most – would draw the line at the rigorous self-discipline and order of life which his 'Spiritual Exercises' require. What we need to do is to ask how much the benefits of the former depend on the fulfillment of the latter. We are familiar with the saying 'no gain without pain', a dictum readily endorsed by those dieting for a slimmer body, or undergoing cosmetic surgery. Is it really a step too far to accept that in the realm of the spiritual life the same principle might apply? It is true that grace is, in the final analysis, free, yet, as Dietrich Bonhoeffer memorably said, there is no such thing as cheap grace. Someone – in this case Jesus Christ – had to pay the price of it.

The 'old way', what we may call the 'catholic' way, does require of those following it a certain discipline of life. The very word 'discipline' may scare us, but the writer of the Letter to the Hebrews puts it in a rewarding context: 'Now, discipline always seems painful rather than pleasant at the time, but later it yields the peaceful fruit of righteousness to those who have been trained by it' (12.11). It's also important to bear in mind that 'discipline' is a word which carries many sinister overtones, but in fact has the same root as 'discipleship'. It is a way of growth, of learning and discovery. To grow into maturity as Christians, to find that 'peaceful fruit', will take time and make demands of us, but they are at heart the demands of love, not duty. 'We love him, because he first loved us' (John 4.19) – there is no great hardship in pleasing the one we love and who loves us. Christian discipline is in truth love's reward.

What does that mean in practice? Should we all sit down and draw up a rigorous code of conduct, commit ourselves to praying for such and such a period of time each day, fix occasions for fasting and plan a path of penitence? The answer is, all may, some should, none must – the same mantra as we earlier applied to the practice of confession to a priest. The only constraint on us should be the constraint of love. How best can I express my love for Christ? How best can I nurture a sense of the love of God for me? What will do most to make me feel that I am loved and valued by him?

Given that constraint, or rather liberated by those questions, I can then sensitively shape a way of being Christian that is mine, but yet is part of the apostolic way – that is consistent with what my fellow believers have discovered on the same journey through all the centuries of the Church's life. I can review all the elements of that ancient way of discipleship and decide which are the most positive and promising ways for me to 'take up my cross daily' and follow Christ.

The 'spiritual reading' of the Scriptures, the Eucharist, confession and absolution, the witness of the saints and Mary, fasting, imaginative prayer, retreats and pilgrimages – yes, and even a rule of life – can all be reviewed. These and other ways of discipleship have served previous generations of Christians well. Within those rich seams today's Christians, with all their questions, doubts and feelings of anxiety and 'unknowing', can surely mine that refined gold in the discovery of which, the apostle Peter said, may be found 'praise and glory and honour'. Thus the old path can lead us to new blessings.